6 - 17 - 73

From

Bob & Cheri

Fathers Day

9-1-73

The Peter
Prescription

By the Same Author

Prescriptive Teaching

The Peter Principle
(with Raymond Hull)

Individual Instruction

The Peter Prescription

How to Be Creative,
Confident, & Competent

BY

Laurence J. Peter

William Morrow & Company, Inc.
NEW YORK • 1972

Printed in the United States of America.
Library of Congress Catalog Card Number 70-182953

2 3 4 5 75 74 73 72

DEDICATION

to Irene, who typed the manuscript but whose
provocativeness distracted me from writing

to H. Cady, editor, who must bear responsibility
for any errors in this book

to Julius Kane, whose statistical analysis *
proved the scientific validity of the
Peter Principle

to C. Northcote Parkinson, who failed to
appreciate the Peter Principle

to Felice, who really understands

to Howard Stern as a down payment on a
large debt

to John, Edward, Alice, and Margaret, may
they avoid the Final Placement Syndrome

to Auriel Prete, who may not exist at all

to readers of *The Peter Principle* whose questions
inspired the writing of *The Peter Prescription*

* Julius Kane, "Dynamics of the Peter Principle,"
Management Science, Vol. 16, No. 12 (August,
1970).

CONTENTS

My way of joking is to tell the truth.
It's the funniest joke in the world.
                                —G. B. SHAW

Introduction
or
Beyond the Peter Principle

> To err is human, but when the eraser wears out
> ahead of the pencil, you're overdoing it.
> —J. JENKINS

EVER since man invented the wheel he has been the confused victim of the miracles he has wrought. He cultivated the land and produced food in abundance. He harnessed the invisible wind with sails and captured the power of tumbling rapids. He converted the heat of combustion into steam to produce power. He illuminated his world with electricity and advanced into the complexities of electronic communication, nuclear fission, computers, and laser beams. He traveled into space and walked on the moon.

> There has been a lot of progress during my
> lifetime, but I'm afraid it's heading in the
> wrong direction.* —O. NASH

* The quotations may help you to relate new ideas to more familiar thoughts.

> The two most engaging powers of an author are to
> make new things familiar and familiar things new.
> —W. THACKERAY

9

Man has been the confused victim of the miracles he has wrought.

Along with all this glorious achievement man has produced some horrendous incompetence. He developed bureaucracy to the point where achievement of the simplest task requires great amounts of time and effort. He built an elaborate postal system, but today it may take longer to deliver a letter than it did in the days of the pony express. He built jet airliners in which he swiftly spans the ocean only to spend hours circling the airport before landing and discovering that his baggage has flown to a destination of its own. He has waited in line for a taxi while taxis have waited in line for customers. He has tried to phone home, but instead of a dial tone has heard only silence or a recorded message about overloaded circuits. He has boarded commuter trains to be delayed by frequent breakdowns.

At home new appliances fail to operate or fall apart within a few days. Service and repair are long delayed and the appliance when returned to the purchaser is soon inoperable again.

> What we call progress is the exchange of one
> nuisance for another nuisance.
>
> —H. ELLIS

His government has sent him an income-tax form that is so complicated he cannot comprehend the instructions. He reads: "If line 15a is under $5,000 and consisted only of wages subject to withholding and not more than $200 of dividends, interest and non-withheld wages, and you are not claiming any adjustments on line 15b, you can have IRS figure your tax by omitting lines 16, 17, 18, 20, 21, 22, 23, 24, 25, and 26 (but complete line 19)."

As man thinks about his monumental blunders in contrast to his spectacular achievements, he realizes he may become a victim of his own or others' incompetence. In school he languished under a teacher who could not teach. He submitted his automobile to a mechanic who returned it with the original defects and some new ones added. He elected a government that promised a great society but could not even produce a balanced budget.

> With ruin upon ruin, rout on rout,
> Confusion worse confounded.
>
> —J. MILTON

My investigations of this competence-incompetence phenomenon led to my formulation of the Peter Principle:

IN A HIERARCHY EVERY EMPLOYEE TENDS TO
RISE TO HIS LEVEL OF INCOMPETENCE

While doing research on the Peter Principle, I discovered that I had founded a new science, hierarchiology, the study of hierarchies.

Man orders his affairs in hierarchies. His schools are ordered in grades from kindergarten through graduate school. His businesses are operated with employees arranged in order of rank. His government is organized with the taxpayers forming the base of the pyramid and the national leader as the apex. Similarly, the military, fraternal orders, social welfare, sports, and the Mafia are all structured as hierarchies.

Because we work in hierarchies and because so much of our lives is controlled by hierarchies it is essential to our well-being and survival that we understand them.

Each hierarchy consists of an arrangement of ranks, grades, or classes to which the individual may be assigned. If he is competent he may contribute to the positive achievement of mankind. Promotion up the ladder may remove him from this level of competence and place him at his level of incompetence.

For every job that exists in the world there is someone, somewhere, who cannot do it. Given sufficient time and enough promotions, he will arrive eventually at that job and there he will remain, habitually bungling the job, frustrating his coworkers, and eroding the efficiency of the organization.

The Peter Principle is not concerned with the oversight, slip of the tongue, *faux pas,* or the occasional error that can be an embarrassment to any of us. Anyone can make a mistake. The most competent men throughout history have had their lapses. Conversely, the habitually incompetent can, by random action, be right once in a while.

> I will not quarrel with a slight mistake,
> Such as our nature's frailty may excuse.
> —EARL OF ROSCOMMON

Although all consistent achievement is the product of those who have not yet reached Final Placement, everyone is subject to the influences of the Peter Principle. All are latent promotees. As numbers of individuals arrive at their levels of incompetence, deadwood accumulates, inefficient bureaucracies grow, quality deteriorates, mediocrity triumphs, companies fail, governments fall, civilization crumbles, and the promise of man's future is obscured.

> It is a paradox that in our time of drastic rapid change, when the future is in our midst devouring the present before our eyes, we have never been less certain about what is ahead of us.
>
> —E. HOFFER

Following the publication of *The Peter Principle*, I received thousands of letters from victims of the Peter Principle requesting solutions to personal problems. At the conclusion of my lectures I was always asked for remedies for specific problems. All of the requests fell into two general categories: (1) What can I do to avoid the Final Placement Syndrome? (2) As a manager, how can I keep my employees at their appropriate competence level? This book, *The Peter Prescription*, was written in response to those questions.

> The real purpose of books is to trap the mind into doing its own thinking.
>
> —C. MORLEY

Many authors offer answers before they understand the questions. This is not the case with the Peter Prescription. I understand the operation of the Peter Principle, and the remedies offered are the product of years of research. I do not always recommend the easiest course of action, but the prescriptions will lead to great personal fulfillment and the joy of real accomplishment.

> There is always an easy solution to every human problem—neat, plausible, and wrong.
>
> —H. L. MENCKEN

The purpose of the Peter Prescription is the achievement of happiness in all aspects of life. This is accomplished through self-actualization or through fulfilling your best potential while avoiding the pitfalls of incompetence. This can be stated very simply:

PETER PRESCRIPTION: FORWARD TO A BETTER LIFE

True progress is achieved through moving forward—not through moving upward to incompetence. *The Peter Prescription* will reveal that your path to real success lies ahead and is achieved through creating a better life rather than climbing upward to total life incompetence. The Peter Prescription replaces mindless escalation with life-quality improvement.

> I will go anywhere provided it is forward.
> —D. LIVINGSTONE

. . . through fulfilling your best potential while avoiding the pitfalls of incompetence.

The Peter Prescription is presented in three parts:

Part One—Incompetence Treadmill

This section will advance your knowledge of the evils wrought by the Peter Principle and give you a clear understanding of why most conventional attempts at solutions only serve to escalate the problems.

Part Two—Protect Your Competence

Your study of this section will show you how to be creative, confident, and competent in your own life. It will show you how to prevent yourself from becoming a tragic victim of mindless escalation and provide you with guidelines for achieving happiness in your private life and satisfaction in your career.

Part Three—Manage for Competence

This section will show you how to be successful in your dealings with others and how to increase your efficiency and competence as a manager.

> We have modified our environment so radically that we must now modify ourselves to exist in this new environment.
> —N. WIENER

PART ONE

Incompetence Treadmill

Brutes find out where their talents lie;
A bear will not attempt to fly,
A foundered horse will oft debate
Before he tries a five barred gate.
A dog by instinct turns aside
Who sees the ditch too deep and wide,
But man we find the only creature
Who, led by folly, combats nature;
Who, when she loudly cries—Forbear!
With obstinacy fixes there;
And where the genius least inclines,
Absurdly bends his whole designs.
—J. SWIFT

CHAPTER I

Onward and Upward
or
Up, Up, and Oops!

> Who soars too near the sun
> with golden wings,
> Melts them; to ruin his own
> fortune brings.
> —W. SHAKESPEARE

WHEN a man is frustrated in his attempt to achieve a goal one of his first responses is to escalate his input— put more money into the project, assign more men to the task, expend more energy or devote more time to the job.

> Accurst ambition,
> How dearly I have bought you.
> —J. DRYDEN

Moe Gull,* a competent chef with a sensitive palate, developed some exquisite recipes for fish chowder. He opened a small restaurant in an attractive old building near a shopping and business center. The day that Moe

---

* Consistent with the successful policy† followed in *The Peter Principle*, names used in the reported case studies are, unless otherwise indicated,‡ fictitious in order to protect the guilty.

† I have not been sued.

‡ "Dr. Laurence J. Peter" is used herein to refer to a real person.

19

Gull's Chowder House opened, it appeared that his modest advertising in the local paper had paid off. Business was
brisk and compliments were many. At the end of the first
six months of business, Moe was taking stock of his adventure in private enterprise. He enjoyed running the
business himself. He personally opened the door in the
morning and closed it again at night. He bought the clams
and fish from a supplier he trusted. He felt confident that
the meals listed on his modest menu were of high quality.
He was proud of the comfortable appearance and cozy
atmosphere of his dining room. His patrons regarded him
as a friend. When a regular patron, Monty Carlo, arrived
at closing time he explained to Moe that he had come all
the way across town for a bowl of Moe's savory chowder.
The traffic had caused a delay. "Too bad," he said. "I
guess I'll have to come back some other time."

Moe said, "Not at all, Monty, come on in. If you don't
mind us cleaning up while you have your dinner, I will
serve you right away." Monty was profuse in his expression of appreciation.

Moe was in absolute control of the business and felt
that decisions were based on his own judgment of each
situation. He regularly experienced the joy of accomplishment and the glow of satisfaction.

Two weeks later Monty Carlo told Moe about a golden
opportunity. The owner of a restaurant with a good location on the other side of town was planning to retire.
Monty was confident that Moe could obtain the business,
including the fixtures and equipment, for a reasonable
price. He insisted that Moe look into it.

Shortly thereafter Moe opened Chowder House Number
2. He tried to supervise the expanded operation by being
in restaurant Number 1 in the mornings and Number 2 in
the afternoons.

What did Moe do about the periods when he was away from each restaurant? Did he tell the chef and waitresses to run things as they saw fit? He did not! He made rules! He made rules about purchasing, then discovered that in an emergency, because of the rules, food could not be obtained from the most available supplier. He solved this by making more rules to cover emergencies. He made rules about promptness and about closing time. When Monty Carlo arrived again just at closing time he was refused service. When he objected to this offhand treatment of a friend who was responsible for expansion of the business, Moe explained that it was a rule and that enforcement of the rules was the only way he could keep control of his business. Monty remarked that it did not matter anyway as Moe Gull's Chowder House had lost its personal touch, had abandoned its quality service, and that the chowder had lost its savor.

By the time Moe Gull had opened two more restaurants he was unable to spend much time in direct supervision. Because of his longer periods of absence from the restaurants, more problems came up when he was away. In order to cope with this he made more rules to cover these contingencies.

As the restaurant chain developed and Moe Gull was not in the restaurants at all, every branch was run by rules. Supplies were ordered through a central office. Procedures were standardized. Restaurant Number 1 became the smallest operation in an expanding bureaucracy.

Three-quarters of the people who work for Moe Gull are not really in the restaurant business. They are nothing more than rule enforcers or rule followers. There is a more serious side effect, though, to bureaucracy than rule enforcing and rule following. Somewhere in this process of escalation of rules, forms, and standardized procedures,

Moe Gull has lost control of his business. The rules he made, in order to keep control, have taken over for themselves.

I will spare you the sordid details of what actually happened as Moe Gull Enterprises expanded and the restaurants deteriorated into just another chain of standard eateries with easily identified façades. Everyone could recognize the giant rotating illuminated plastic chowder bowls on the rooftops of all the Moe Gull Restaurants. They could rely on the standard menus and dull unchanging synthetic meals. There was no surprise in store for Moe Gull's patrons. Everything possible was standardized. Now Moe, the organization man, spends his working day as the chief executive administering his empire.

> The slave has but one master, the ambitious man has as many masters as there are persons whose aid may contribute to the advancement of his fortune.
>
> —J. DE LA BRUYÈRE

Excessive escalation can result in pollution of any system. A single human organism can overconsume the best of nutritious life-sustaining food and develop indigestion or obesity that will impair his health and endanger his life. Excessive use of internal-combustion engines can pollute the atmosphere. The right amount of fertilizer added to the soil will increase productivity whereas excessive amounts may be harmful. Escalation of the production and use of pesticides can poison the environment and kill essential insects, fish, birds, and animals and upset the balance of nature's cycles. Escalation of human and industrial waste in our once crystal lakes and streams can turn them into open cesspools. Escalation can convert the affluent society into the effluent society.

Pollution can be the result of excessive noxious matter

A single human organism can overconsume the best of nutritious, life-sustaining food.

that poisons the system, or it can result from mindless escalation of something which in appropriate quantities was beneficial. It can be simply too much of a good thing.

> A surfeit of the sweetest things,
> The deepest loathing to the stomach brings.
> —W. Shakespeare

One form of pollution that has not received sufficient attention from social ecologists is caused by bureaucratic escalation. Just as air and water pollution create an unfavorable physical environment, organizational pollution can create an unfavorable social environment. Victims of pollution of the physical environment are often unaware that they are being poisoned until it is too late. This occurs because the build-up is gradual and the lethal dose is not easily detected. Similarly, in the case of *bureaucratic pollution,* red tape gradually accumulates; until the fatal day arrives when an organization is helplessly strangled. Some government agencies that originally produced a useful service now produce only forms and procedures for processing the forms they produce. For all practical purposes the agency has died from red-tape poisoning.

Even though rules and regulations are essential for the protection of the individual and for the well-being of the society, escalation of bureaucracy can unnecessarily harass, stifle, and corrupt individuals and undermine the health of society. It is overescalation and overofficiousness of bureaucracy that destroy the social system.

> There is little to admire in bureaucracy, but you've got to hand it to the Internal Revenue Service.
>
> —J. L. ROGERS

Today bureaucrats exist in abundance in every hierarchy of government, the military, education, and business. Unfortunately the individual bureaucrat is not readily recognizable. He may spend a lifetime in his pursuit of duty without anyone recognizing what he is about. In other cases he may prefer the blatant badge of authority and insist that he is only carrying out the rules.

> There is only one giant machine operated by pygmies, and that is bureaucracy.
>
> —H. DE BALZAC

Bureaucratic pollution may cost you your freedom as the hierarchy invades your privacy and takes over more and more of your life. Excessive escalation of the military establishment may produce a gigantic hierarchy that consumes a major part of your tax dollar, yet may provide little real defense. As a matter of fact the military bureaucracy, originally established to protect your freedom, may be escalated to become the invader of your privacy, the controller of your taxes, the destroyer of your freedom.

Nations are quite capable of starving every
other side of life—education, sanitation, hous-
ing, public health, everything that contributes
to life, physical, intellectual, moral, and spirit-
ual—in order to maintain their armaments.
—G. L. DICKINSON

Excessive escalation of the educational or welfare establishment may not solve the problems of ignorance or
poverty, yet you will have to pay the bill.

Bureaucratic pollution weakens the function of government and the victims may never know what is truly the
matter. The point at which a system takes control for itself
is the point at which the social ecological balance is upset.
At this point the bureaucracy escalates automatically and
rules, regulations, and rituals become hopelessly entrenched.

The inflexibility of the bureaucracy becomes terrifying
as it entraps us on a course and keeps us there no matter
what. Men of vision who see the inflexibility of the
bureaucratic system try to rescue us from this social ecological disaster. Unfortunately, they discover that government bureaucracies will tolerate creativity or innovation
only within bureaucratically established guidelines.

Bureaucracy defends the status quo long past
the time when the quo has lost its status.
—L. PETER

With each day that passes we have less and less chance
to determine our destiny. The preservation of the status
quo makes change of direction impossible. We are
hemmed in and are unable to change direction even
when circumstances demand it.

With so many tragic examples of individuals devoting

*Excessive accumulation of material goods imposes
unwanted responsibility.*

their lives to struggling up the hierarchy only to realize
that vast wealth does not produce happiness, that excessive accumulation of material goods imposes unwanted
responsibility, and that high office involves burdensome
pressures and conflicts, why does man still escalate?

> Ah! curst ambition! to thy lures we owe
> All the great ills that mortals bear below.
> —A. THIRKELL

CHAPTER II

Sex and Society
or
Life After Birth

"My dear, we live in a time of transition,"
said Adam as he led Eve out of Paradise.
—W. INGE

THE Peter Principle explains how men and women, in established hierarchies, climb the ladder of success until they arrive at their respective levels of incompetence. Where an established hierarchy is not readily available, the individual soon builds one and starts his ascent. Nowhere is this more evident than in human social and sexual behavior.

Most hierarchies were established by men. The church, business, education, and the military each established its male hierarchal structure before women obtained the right to participate.

As women entered and ascended these established hierarchies they became victims in the same way men do. For example, the invention of the typewriter established a new profession for women in the business world. It was not long before some of these women became secretaries and office managers. Men who established the hierarchies also established a mythology that women were constitutionally ill-equipped for the top executive positions. This created prejudice that prevented some women from rising to their levels of incompetence and resulted in male executives having a monopoly on stress-induced neuroses, coronaries, alcoholism, and gastric ulcers. Today, as women are moving toward equality of opportunity, many are falling victim to the same stress diseases.

> A woman has to be twice as good as a man to go half as far.
>
> —F. HURST

Although the sexual revolution, women's liberation movement, and late-late television have altered the human sexual response, marriage still appears to be a way of life for many.

> You marry the person who is available when you are most vulnerable.
>
> —K. BERWICK

Do you wonder why so many married couples find themselves to be incompatible? Do you sometimes catch yourself suspecting your mate of infidelity? Do you wonder about your husband's inconsistency when he stays after hours at a job he claims to detest? Do you grow impatient because you are not advancing to the social status of the couple next door?

These are matters of vital interest in millions of homes each day. They are symptomatic of a basic pitfall in marital life—one which can be viewed rationally only through the perspective of the Peter Principle.

The marital corollary to the Peter Principle is that "In marriage, mates tend to create their own hierarchies and eventually escalate their social and sexual expectations to levels they are incompetent to attain."

> What is irritating about love is that it is a crime that requires an accomplice.
>
> —C. BAUDELAIRE

*Do you sometimes catch yourself suspecting
your mate of infidelity?*

Did you ever wonder whether Cinderella and the charming prince really did "live happily ever after" as the fairy tale suggests? A more probable version of their marital outcome is that they were miserable together. In other words, Cinderella's fairy godmother * was really a villain, not a godsend.

By transforming Cinderella temporarily from rags to riches and winning for her the young prince, the fairy godmother escalated Cinderella beyond the limits of her social competence. The prince, it turned out, was really no more than a typical royal playboy, and he soon grew tired of Cinderella's peasant mannerisms once he had satisfied his playboy instinct. Unfortunately for Cinderella, social competence in the cultured ways of the king's court did not descend upon her just because she married royalty. She soon fell out of favor with the prince's family and friends. The more Cinderella was criticized about her uncourtly ways, the more miserable the prince made life for her. Their marriage was doomed to failure.

Cinderella had been deceived by her fairy godmother. She had accepted instant escalation and had arrived overnight at her level of incompetence. She would have been happier had she married a handsome young woodcutter and found fulfillment at her level of social competence.

We can conclude that moving up the social ladder, whether intentionally or not, was a curse in the days of royal courts, knighthood, and chivalry, but the marital hierarchy still exists today.

> Bride: a woman with a fine prospect of happiness behind her.
>
> —A. BIERCE

Kathy Coed was a blond bombshell who had received a modern-dance scholarship to prestigious Status State Col-

* Probably promoted from Tooth Fairy.

lege. Despite her lower-class background she used her beauty to move up socially as president of the school's most promiscuous sorority. She flirted with football players on the college team but found them to be unsophisticated by the standards she was steadily picking up from her wealthy sorority sisters. When she finally met S. Cholar, Phi Beta Kappa captain of the college debate squad, she fell for him immediatcly.

But when she became Mrs. S. Cholar, Kathy found that her good looks alone were not enough for her truly sophisticated husband. He became displeased with her childish giggling and her full-time preoccupation with shopping for new clothes. Kathy, unablc to adapt to a scholarly life style of inconspicuous consumption, soon began flirting with the plumber. The S. Cholars' marriage went quickly down the drain.

> If ambition doesn't hurt you, you haven't got it.
> —K. NORRIS

The wealthy parents of Alice Nobb had sent her to Status State College with the hope that she would find a well-to-do student for a husband. Alice decided she could do better by attracting B. Hefty, a 250-pound football player who was taking business-administration courses to maintain his athletic scholarship. Alice figured Hefty could provide her with wealth and status as a professional football player before retiring into business. So they were married while still in college.

As it turned out, the promising Hefty was injured in his final college game. He then discovered that no professional team wanted him, and business firms that previously had competed for the college hero's services now used his poor grades as an excuse for their lack of interest in him.

Needless to say, Alice did not attain the wcalth or status she and her parents had hoped for. She was stuck with a

250-pound used-car salesman, and she began to blame him for her absence from social circles.

In my studies, brides have revealed countless ingenious ways of creating hierarchies and escalating their marital ambitions beyond their grasp.

A man's home is his hassle.
—Mrs. L. Peter

Mr. and Mrs. S. P. Oyl lived an unextravagant but happy life for ten years in an old apartment house. Then Mrs. Oyl inherited several valuable paintings from an aunt in France. She decided to impress her fellow tenants by decorating her apartment with the paintings. She soon found that the paintings looked out of place in the shabby surroundings and so bought an Oriental rug to set them off. Still unsatisfied, she spent the family's small savings on European furniture to enhance the carpet and paintings.

Once-friendly neighbors began to feel uneasy when visiting the elegant apartment. They resented Mrs. Oyl's showiness, and declined her invitations. She in turn began to resent her friends for their lack of appreciation of the better things of life. She convinced her husband that the neighborhood was too low-brow for cultured people like the Oyls, and so they moved uptown into a penthouse apartment. Since Mr. Oyl now had to work overtime to afford a penthouse, he often came home exhausted and disgruntled. Mrs. Oyl began seeing him as an uncultured slob who did not belong in the newly acquired artistic surroundings, so she divorced him and married a more suitable man.

The cultured gentleman she married, Art E. Apex, did not take long to see through her shallow pretension to sophistication and art appreciation. He began to mistreat her, much as she had abused her former husband. Mrs. Apex was miserable, having built her own hierarchy and climbed from happiness to tragedy.

> Love is an ideal thing, marriage a real thing; a confusion of the real with the ideal never goes unpunished.
>
> —J. GOETHE

What do these cases have in common? Where did the couples go wrong? They all tried to achieve happiness through escalation. Had they remained at more realistic levels of financial, social, and sexual competence, they could have remained comfortably below their levels of incompetence and achieved fulfillment through strengthening their sexual and interpersonal relationships.

Before the discovery of the Peter Principle, escalation was considered profitable. Accumulating wealth, power, and social prestige was thought to be a virtue. Becoming a member of high society was a valued goal. Acquiring a prestigious sexual or marital partner was a worthwhile achievement.

Although today's divorce courts are full of couples who escalated to marital incompetence, few can compare with the unsuccessful marriages of England's Henry VIII, two of whose wives paid the maximum price for having over-escalated in order to marry a king.

Today only a few marriages end that drastically. Marriages that begin successfully and end tragically frequently result from the Beverly Hillbillies Complex: the universal propensity of men and women to seek entrance into social circles beyond their background and social competence.

Fortunately it is possible to avoid your level of marital incompetence. Love and sharing in marriage are fulfillment; ambition and escalation are a trap.

Ambition is a lust that's never quenched,
Grows more inflamed, and madder by enjoy-
ment.

—T. OTWAY

Otto Workman, a competent mechanic at G. Rhyme
Auto Repair Company, was satisfied with his job because
it required little paper work. When he was offered a promotion to an administrative position with the company,
he was tempted to decline. His wife, Winnie, an active
member of the local Women's Social Betterment League,
urged him to accept the promotion. With it, the family
could move up socially and economically, she could run
for the presidency of the W.S.B.L., and they could afford
a new car, a new wardrobe for her, and a mini-motorbike
for their son.

Otto did not want to exchange his current work for
office drudgery, but he succumbed to Winnie's persuasive
nagging and accepted the promotion. Now, six months
later, he has an ulcer. His doctor has ordered him to quit
drinking. Winnie accuses Otto of having an affair with his
new secretary and of costing her the Women's Social Betterment League presidency. Otto puts in long hours at
frustrating work and is irritable when he gets home each
night. The Workmans' marriage is no longer working.

Man has made his bedlam; let him lie in it.

—F. ALLEN

A. Trueheart, a competent coworker of Workman's at
G. Rhyme Auto Repair Company, had also been considered for a promotion. But his wife, Sally, understood
that he enjoyed his current job and would not want to be
tied up with the extra hours and responsibilities of an
office job. She did not try to force him to accept a promotion he would not like, and he remained a competent
mechanic—leaving the ulcers to Workman.

Trueheart maintained his sunny disposition and remained a popular fellow in the neighborhood, where he served as a youth leader in his spare time. The neighbors responded by bringing their cars to the G. Rhyme Auto Repair Company. Trueheart's employers realized the great asset they had in him and gave him a bonus, steady employment, and all the wage increments permissible within the schedule. Trueheart was able to buy a new family car, a new wardrobe for Sally, and a bicycle and baseball glove for their son. The Truehearts live a comfortable and satisfying life. Their successful marriage is the envy of their friends and neighbors, and they have more community prestige than Mrs. Workman ever hoped for.

> Find where your main roots lie and do not
> hanker after other worlds.
> —H. THOREAU

The Masculine Mystique

Since automation and the electronic revolution, men are not only working fewer hours, but are also engaged in more activities where physical prowess, strength, and stamina are unimportant. They are being paid more for less physical work performed in fewer hours than ever before. This causes anxiety and frustration. They feel guilty and uncomfortable because this is the opposite of what they have been taught. They have been brought up to believe that self-worth is only possible by hard, painstaking work. Automation is in direct conflict with the Puritan ethic and is causing men to lose self-esteem.

> Striving to better, oft we mar what's well.
> —W. SHAKESPEARE

The male ego has not only been dealt a severe blow by the electronic revolution, it has been buffeted by the communications revolution and stomped upon by the feminist movement. Advertising and television have caricatured man as an incompetent schnook. The formula is: Women are smarter than men, children are smarter than women, animals are smarter than children. The unfortunate male who has lost his identity and has been ridiculed by the communications media now finds that his masculine preserves are being invaded by women. In defeat he tries to be polite about it. His chivalry is rebuffed and he is called a male chauvinist pig. He tries to retain his masculine self-concept, but his attempts at romance brand him as a sexist female-exploiting dog.

In a society based on marriage, why do so many men remain bachelors? To find the complete answer we must add to the reasons given above the fact that the female matures earlier than the male. This complicates the problem of finding the right girl. It is easy to find a girl and to fall in love when a man is young. The urge is strong, the sap is high, and the powers of selectivity are undeveloped.

> The girl who is easy to get may be hard to take.
>
> —F. Wisely

There are some men who do not fall in love and some who keep falling in love but do not marry. As a man matures sooner or later he reaches the age of discretion. The blood ceases to boil and reason takes over. Instead of rushing into marriage he considers the evidence for and against. After a man reaches a certain age, marriage decreases in value. The urgent appetite for sex decreases. He is now experienced at satisfying his needs without benefit of marriage. He still wants sex, but the price he will pay has slumped.

A bachelor does not grow lonelier as the years pass by. He learns how to live with himself. He satisfies his unique social needs. His companions may consist of members of

He still wants sex, but the price he will pay has slumped.

his own sex or of the opposite sex or any combination of
the above. He may dream of the exceptional girl who
could excite him to the point where he would give up all
this, but while his standards are going up, the quality of
what he can get is going down. The available choice of
desirable prospective wives gets smaller day by day. As
his competence in making a rational selection increases,
the desirable selectees decrease.

To estimate his chances of success he looks at his married pals. Most are stalking girls at the office or sneaking
off with others' wives. He concludes that if married men
have mistresses or look for sex and love outside of marriage he would not improve his situation by wedlock. A
bachelor is a man who looks before he leaps—and then
does not leap.

> Bachelors know more about women than mar-
> ried men; if they didn't, they'd be married, too.
>   —H. L. Mencken

The Feminine Mistake

Man has escalated himself to his level of incompetence and established military, industrial, and social hierarchies that may bring the progress of civilization to a halt or even destroy the human race. The establishment of the institutions that produced this disastrous state has been primarily a masculine activity. The executive positions within these hierarchies have been occupied predominantly by men. Although men have dominated in total life incompetence, it could not have occurred without the support of their helpmates. American women, for example, own more than 50 percent of the money in the country. They have 65 percent of the savings accounts and control 57 percent of listed securities. They have title to 74 percent of suburban homes, and control 87½ percent of total buying power.

The Peter Principle describes the cause-and-effect relationship between man's hierarchal escalation and his incompetence. It does not deny his right to become incompetent. It would be equally unfair to deny women their right to become victims of the Peter Principle.

> No person should be denied equal rights because of the shape of her skin.
>
> —P. PAULSEN

The equalization of opportunity for the sexes could result in women becoming equally incompetent to men. If women liberationists accept their share of all jobs, they may free men from such formerly all-male entrapments as coal miner, subway builder, cargo loader, heavyweight boxer, sewer worker, and army draftee. This will only mean that more men and women will be available to achieve higher levels of incompetence and further endanger the peace and safety of the world.

If women liberationists strive to become bank presidents, chief executives of the political-industrial complex, and Navy admirals, Army generals, and flight commanders, they will inevitably add to the total life incompetence of civilized society.

> America is the only matriarchy where women
> are fighting for equality.
>
>   —A. ROTH

Should the liberated woman seek equality with the male incompetent incumbents and join in a battle of the sexes on the treadmill to oblivion, or should she accept the Peter Prescription and assume leadership in a movement toward a better world? Should she dare to be the

Should the liberated woman seek equality?

supercompetent who abandons the hierarchal strugggle and sets new directions toward improvement of the quality of life in a cleaner, more peaceful, and beautiful land?

> Man's world is in trouble, and in spite of this, women are hell-bent to get out into it and go to work on its problems!
>
> —E. JANEWAY

CHAPTER III

Hierarchal Regression
or
Your Ladder Is Slipping

> Ours is the age which is proud of machines that
> think, and suspicious of men who try to.
> —H. MUMFORD JONES

W HEN I first wrote about the Peter Principle, I assumed it applied to all or at least most professions, but I
could not be certain. Although it was impossible for me
to study every organization that existed in the world, the
ones I investigated conformed to the Principle.

> Make three correct guesses consecutively and
> you will establish a reputation as an expert.
> —L. PETER

Shortly after publication of the Peter Principle articles
I was invited to present a lecture to the faculty and graduate students of the School of Business Administration at
a major university. My first reaction was one of astonish-
ment. Why would these experts in administration want to
hear from me? I expressed my amazement to the dean of
Business Administration but was assured that the program
committee had requested my lecture. Two days later a
delegation of four graduate students appeared at my office for an interview. During the short conversation that

41

ensued I was led to believe that the dean had not read the Peter Principle articles and that if he had read them he would have opposed my presentation. The delegation insisted that the dean was the ultimate case of the Horatio Alger Complex. His office walls were decorated with such signs as ONWARD AND UPWARD, HE WHO HESITATES IS LOST, and WHERE THERE'S A WILL THERE'S A WAY.

At the appointed time I appeared at the Business Administration Building and began my search for the assigned lecture room. There was no directory in evidence in the foyer, so I began an exploration of the halls and byways. The room numbers provided no guidance as they appeared to be randomly assigned. On a nearby bulletin board, in a montage of misinformation dating back to the dedication of the building, I discovered three notices regarding my lecture. One described the location as Room 5, another Room 25, and a third as the auditorium in the Home Economics Building. As I stood before this tacky tackboard, contemplating the conflicting information and the whimsical room-numbering system, I became aware of another bulletin-board reader. He, too, was looking for the Peter Principle lecture. We set off together to continue the search. Others joined us en route. We encountered searchers hurrying in various directions announcing that the lecture was in the seminar room, the auditorium, and the students' lounge. Several faculty members, each with a delegation of students in tow, moved from room to room in search of the lecture. I was advised not to worry because mix-ups like this occurred quite frequently. No group large enough to qualify as a quorum alighted in one room long enough for me to begin the lecture.

Was the School of Business Administration a pure expression of the Peter Principle? Had these administration experts reached their level of administrative incompetence? How could they teach others the art of administration if they could not administer their own school of administration? Other questions crossed my mind. Had the committee underestimated the dean? Had he read *The Peter Principle?* Had he practiced Creative Incompetence to keep me from speaking?

> The university brings out all abilities including incapability.
>
> —A. CHEKHOV

In the months that followed I accepted many speaking assignments and addressed large groups of experts. The information I received regarding the annual convention of a society of industrial engineers contained a detailed history of the organization but failed to inform me about the location of the meeting. The brochure describing a conference of management consultants stated that the

*In the months that followed I accepted
many speaking assignments.*

meeting was to be held at 2:00 P.M. but failed to indicate
the date. Timing was the theme of an international workshop of systems analysts. My lecture was scheduled for
3:00 P.M. and the conference was to close at 4:00 P.M.
Each speaker emphasized the importance of accurate time
schedules and each spoke far beyond his allotted time.
I was finally introduced at 4:25 P.M. Although I was in the
hands of experts, there was no way in which I could finish
my speech by 4:00 P.M. on that day. At other meetings I
listened to dull, boring speeches on the subject of motivation and lectures about the ineffectiveness of lectures.

> MURPHY'S LAW:
> (1) Nothing is as easy as it looks.
> (2) Everything takes longer than you think.
> (3) If anything can go wrong, it will.

These experiences, augmented by interviews with a
variety of business consultants, produced overwhelming
evidence that although many business consultants were
competent, a substantial number were victims of the Peter
Principle. These experts had reached their professional
status through escalation—the same route their clients had
utilized in achieving the incompetence the experts were
supposed to cure.

> An expert is one who knows more and more
> about less and less.
>
> —N. BUTLER

My investigations disclosed that some competent management researchers were aware that many consultants
were incompetent. Although they recognized the problem, their advice was somewhat lacking in logic. They
suggested that the manager in need of expert help should
evaluate the consultant's qualifications and competence
before engaging him. A manager having problems in a
specific area of his business is probably the least qualified

to evaluate the competence of an expert in that specific area.

Management consultants are the doctors of the business world. They are called in to solve managerial problems, to revitalize defunct businesses, and to maximize efficiency. Management consultants are generally recruited from academic and professional ranks, and in most cases becoming a business consultant is regarded as a promotion. The range of expertise offered by management consultants is growing rapidly. From a handful of efficiency experts the consulting profession has grown in the United States to become a billion-dollar industry of more than 2,700 firms. The experts are now called industrial engineers, systems analysts, consulting management engineers, and so forth.

> Most universities have faculty members on their staff who, particularly in the area of business and scientific technologies, make more from part-time consulting work than they do from their professional salaries.
>
> —H. Higdon

The indiscriminate escalation of the number of consultants offers no assurance of competence. The attempt to produce competence through escalation of consultation holds no more promise of success than does any other form of escalation.

> Even when the experts all agree, they may well be mistaken.
>
> —B. Russell

Peter Route, a productive idea man in the design department at Super Sales and Solicitations, was made manager of the Promotion Development Department.

In this new position he still generates ideas at a prodigious rate but unfortunately lacks the patience needed to schedule, supervise, and evaluate the work of his pedestrian staff. Peter Route dazzles everyone with his wit and brilliance but his enthusiasm for each project is short-lived. The outcome of his promotion is a deterioration of efficiency.

> Irresolution on the schemes of life which offer themselves to our choice, and inconstancy in pursuing them, are the greatest causes of all our unhappiness.
>
> —J. ADDISON

At Super Sonic Zeppelin Corporation it was decided that two employees, Hans Zup and Gustav Wind, were hindering the smooth operation of the organization.

When Hans Zup was a supervisor in the plant, his amiable easygoing manner had contributed to effective personnel relations. When he was promoted to superintendent he still gave in to everybody. It was realized that Hans Zup had reached his level of incompetence through a real promotion. The decision was made to give him a pseudo promotion—to kick him upstairs. This percussive sublimation was accomplished by creating a new post, that of Vice President in Charge of Jurisdictional Protocol and Company History. Hans Zup has been replaced in the active hierarchy by a competent superintendent and the organization has been restored to normal.

It was feared that Gustav Wind's aggressive manner with government officials might have some negative repercussions at a time when Super Sonic Zeppelin was dependent upon government subsidies to keep it afloat. Gustav was given a pseudo promotion to remove him from the active hierarchy. This was accomplished by appointing him to the office of Deputy Associate Assistant Co-Chairman, Committee on Innovation.

> A committee is a group of the unprepared, appointed by the unwilling, to do the unnecessary.
>
> —F. ALLEN

The effectiveness of any hierarchy is adversely influenced by each individual who reaches his office of incapacity. Occasionally this situation is remedied through removal of the incumbent by dismissal or by a pseudo promotion. If this is done promptly the hierarchy may recover and suffer no permanent damage.

> To err is human, and so is trying to avoid correcting it.
> —R. REYCRAFT

The effectiveness of a hierarchy or of any office within a hierarchy depends upon its skill and its reputation. Skill is its actual competence in achieving its objectives. Reputation is its relationship with the public. The combined interrelationship of skill and reputation produces the real status of the hierarchy.

> If you respect your job's importance, it will probably return the favor.
> —L. D. TURNER

Years ago many of the students at Excelsior City College graduated to become competent employees in the offices of the Excelsior Mattress Company. Excelsior Mattress thought well of Excelsior College so Excelsior graduates received preferential treatment as applicants for employment and promotion.

In those simpler times the Excelsior School System was a stable hierarchy, a pure expression of the Peter Principle. Pupils progressed from grade to grade or from competence to competence. Each pupil was promoted until he reached his level of incompetence. Then he was said to have "failed" the grade. He would then "repeat the grade," or if he was of age he could leave school and find employment at a manual job. This was the way things worked back in the days when teachers were in charge of the schools.

The establishment of graduate schools of education and escalation within the education profession resulted in educationists gaining control of the schools. Before this happened it was believed that a teacher was someone who could understand those not very good at explaining and explain to those not very good at understanding. Today the educationist is someone who can take an easy subject and make it difficult.

When educationists gained dominance of the schools they convinced the teachers that their promotion policy was psychologically unsound. The educationists favored a plan called social promotion, in which the competent as well as the incompetent were promoted. Standards declined. Remedial reading courses became a necessity in universities and "Beverly Hillbillies" became a top-rated television program.

> An expert is a man who has stopped thinking—
> he knows.
>
> —F. LLOYD WRIGHT

The Status Account

Landing on the moon has proved a triumph of American technology, yet here on American soil nothing seems to work properly any more. You can list dozens of examples of incompetence from your own experience: defective merchandise, carelessness of sales and service personnel, bungling by bureaucrats, mistakes of computers, the laziness of your subordinates, the indecisiveness of your superiors. You are surrounded, bedeviled, persecuted by incompetence from the cradle to the grave.

> If there's anything a public servant hates to do
> it's something for the public.
>
> —K. HUBBARD

Each new hierarchy initially produces considerable competence but eventually matures into a bureaucracy of ineptitude. Each has its day before it deteriorates into dynamic inactivism. Postal and telegraph systems, railroads, telephone monopolies, airlines, gas and electric utilities—each was a shining example of competence before *Hierarchal Regression* set in.

> Technological progress has merely provided us
> with more efficient means for going backwards.
> —A. Huxley

Each office within a hierarchy has a status account to which the occupant makes deposits or withdrawals. The balance fluctuates. In a new hierarchy, rapid expansion, youth, and creativity result in a high degree of competence. Mobility permits talent to be applied where needed. During this period the status of each office occupied by a competent will increase in proportion to the competence deposit made by that occupant. If a succession of competents occupy the office its status will continue to grow. If the majority of offices within a hierarchy each develop a healthy status balance the entire hierarchy experiences status rise. This is what happened to our major institutions early in their development.

As hierarchies matured the effect of the Peter Principle became evident. Bureaucratic pollution limited the effectiveness of the competent individuals while it protected the incompetence of those who had achieved final placement. Each incompetent made a withdrawal from the status account of the office he occupied. A succession of incompetents bankrupted the status account. In time the total hierarchy regressed.

> When everyone is somebody then no one's anybody.
> —W. Gilbert

Unfortunately we are living in a time when many of our major institutions are suffering from Hierarchal Regression and the status of government, the church, education, the military, business, and industry is seriously depleted.

> I do not believe in the collective wisdom of individual ignorance.
>
> —T. CARLYLE

Because change is so rapid it is not uncommon for an individual in midcareer to find that the hierarchy is passing him by. In other words, he has climbed part way up the ladder and feels competent. He stops to rest, but rapid technological change goes on. He intends to catch up, but when he tries he is technologically obsolete. He has become uneducated for his job simply by standing still.

> Our Age of Anxiety is, in great part, the result of trying to do today's job with yesterday's tools—with yesterday's concepts.
>
> —M. McLUHAN

A common problem in vocational, social, educational, and other hierarchies is that the individual does not know where he stands. He knows his nominal rank, of course—Assistant Mail Order Shipper, Treasurer of the Community Betterment Association, Eighth Grade Student, or Junior Senator—but that is only his *Apparent Hierarchal Status*. His *Real Hierarchal Status* is his balance in the status account based upon his skill and the reputation of his office.

In an old-fashioned, paternalistic hierarchy, where the boss knew every employee and every employee knew the boss, it was easy to find out just where you stood. The boss smiled at Mr. A as he worked his machine; he stopped and talked to Miss B at the reception desk; he scowled at Mr. C, the maintenance foreman; he occasionally lunched with Mr. D, the head bookkeeper; he invited Sales Manager E to his home for dinner. Each employee could assess his real position by the boss's behavior toward him.

In the old-fashioned school, every pupil in Grade 8 had proved himself competent in Grade 7, so his Apparent Hierarchal Status and his Real Hierarchal Status were identical. Not so nowadays. The trend toward granting social promotions has eroded the significance of the grade system. Apparent Hierarchal Status is no longer equal to Real Hierarchal Status; many pupils are at their level of incompetence, but do not know it.

This is the most significant danger of not knowing where you stand. Unless you know your real position you may be an *Unwitting Incompetent*. As an Unwitting Incompetent you will not know the truth about whether incompetence lies within yourself, within others, or within the system.

Unwitting Incompetence has a serious detrimental effect on the hierarchy. The Unwitting Incompetent cannot fulfill his proper function. He makes a substantial withdrawal from the status account and throws an extra burden upon his competent colleagues. If he is high enough up the hierarchy, he may become part of the expanding deadwood in the executive suite. The actions of a leader suffering from Unwitting Incompetence may so confound the entire organization as to render normally competent subordinates temporarily incompetent. The Unwitting Incompetent at Final Placement can so confuse a subordinate that he simply cannot operate. This *Incompetency Fallout* occurs when the qualified subordinate either becomes immobilized through frustration or voluntarily employs Creative Incompetence when he perceives the futility of attempting to function competently under an Unwitting Incompetent.

The effect of Unwitting Incompetence on the individual

incompetent is slight so long as he continues in blissful ignorance. But if he does find out, he suffers feelings of dismay and shock proportional to the time elapsed since he achieved Final Placement.

JENKINSON'S LAW: It won't work.

For example, Ardleigh Abel achieved his incompetence as Assistant Director in Charge of Public Relations for the Excelsior City Planetarium. Abel's first act was to launch a fund-raising campaign urging citizens to support the planetarium because the prevailing overcast caused by the heavy industries of Excelsior City deprived citizens of a view of the sun by day and the starry sky by night.

Excelsior City Iron Works, Excelsior Oil, and Excelsior Ceramics immediately canceled their annual donations to the planetarium. As other major donors withdrew their support, Abel gradually realized his position and began to be paranoid about the security of his files and compulsively neurotic about the neatness and arrangement of his desk—symptoms of the Final Placement Syndrome.

> Only a mediocre person is always at his best.
> —S. MAUGHAM

We have seen that the status of the total hierarchy can fluctuate and the tendency is toward Hierarchal Regression. We have also seen that the individual may not be aware of his Real Hierarchal Status and may even be an Unwitting Incompetent. These factors contribute to change that is not true progress. Progress always means change, but change does not always mean progress. Driving manners become more crude as gasoline becomes more refined. Man flies to the moon safely but crosses the street at his peril.

> Civilization is a limitless multiplication of unnecessary necessities. —M. TWAIN

Only a mediocre person is always at his best.

Computerized Incompetence

Charles Babbage,* an English mathematician of the nineteenth century, was the engineering genius who invented the speedometer and the cowcatcher. He once wrote to Lord Tennyson:

> Sir, in your otherwise beautiful poem
> "The Vision of Sin" there is a verse
> which reads
> > Every moment dies a man,
> > Every moment one is born.
> It must be manifest that if this were
> true, the population of the world would
> be at a standstill. In truth the rate
> of birth is slightly in excess of that

* Not a fictitious name.

of death. I would suggest that in the
next edition of your poem you have it read
    Every moment dies a man,
    Every moment $1\frac{1}{16}$ is born. . . .
I am, Sir, yours, etc.

Is it any wonder that this man is father of the high-speed digital computer? He spent the last four decades of his life engaged in a monumental attempt to build an "Analytical Engine" that would perform every single arithmetical function without any human guidance except the feeding of instructions and the turning of the switch.

The Analytical Engine was fantastically sophisticated in spite of the ungainliness of its gears, levers, and cranks. Like modern computers it consisted of four interconnected sections—a memory bank, a computation section, a control center, and an input-output center. The mechanical monster was programmed with punch cards.

Unfortunately for Babbage, what he needed to make his computer practical was the vacuum tube, which was not invented until 1906. Complex World War II projects stimulated engineering interest in developing a computer, utilizing the vacuum tube, that would handle huge computational jobs at unprecedented speeds. Miniaturization through transistorization has enabled the computer to store incredible quantities of data on tape and small magnetic disks.

> PUDDER'S LAW: Anything that begins well ends badly.

Computers are vulnerable to incompetence in spite of the fact that they seldom make mistakes on their own. The computers are helplessly dependent on the reliability of the information and instructions fed into them. A keypunch operator may make a mistake and you will receive a domestic phone bill for $2,314.69 for the month of July, when you were away on vacation. Unfortunately, the computer has no way of knowing that the key-punch operator had a temporary lapse or that you were on vacation.

> Computers are fantastic: in a few minutes they
> can make a mistake so great that it would take
> many men many months to equal it.
> —M. MEACHAM

The computer, like the human employee, can be promoted from doing the kinds of things it does well to performing the kinds of tasks for which it is unsuitable.

The computer's memory banks and lightning-quick circuitry challenge man's limited quantity of valid data. The quality of data deteriorates, resulting in the familiar phenomenon of GIGO (Garbage In-Garbage Out).

> Computers can figure out all kinds of problems,
> except the things in this world that just don't
> add up.   —J. MAGARY

Because the computer's capability has far outstripped our ability to use it wisely, bureaucrats mindlessly make work for it by designing elaborate forms to collect vast amounts of irrelevant information.

> Lo! Men have become the tools of their tools.
> —H. THOREAU

Man believes that he has designed a machine in his own image. In deluding himself into believing that the prototype is his own brain, he forgets that his brain is not composed of rigidly defined circuits and transistors. He fails to reflect that his brain is a soggy computer in which dynamic chemistry influences every function. His brain may be activated by such external stimuli as a pretty girl or a beautiful sunset, and such internal stimuli as a humanistic impulse or quiet contemplation.

> The brain is better for a writer than a computer.
> —N. WIENER

In earlier times a man had to cut and carry wood and light a fire to warm his house; harness a horse and drive a buggy to go into town; and milk a cow to obtain milk for his family. But at least he had a measure of control over these functions and had the satisfaction of knowing that all systems were operating. Today he has few of these satisfactions—he is humbled by a helpless dependency on complex technology.

Machines that originally made life easy may eventually make life impossible. Computers that have already begun to replace and enslave us may eventually leave us incompetent to do the simple tasks we once did for ourselves.

> As machines get to be more and more like men, men will come to be more and more like machines. —J. KRUTCH

Computer specialists develop a type of tunnel vision consisting of statistical-empirical-digital thinking. These specialists have underdeveloped ability for making sound value judgments and an overdeveloped capacity for digital thinking. Comprehensive value judgments require total system perspective, sustained mental effort, and in-depth analysis. Digital judgments are much simpler and even a wrong decision is impressive as a readout from today's complex equipment.

Modern computer systems are creating a new generation of bureaucrats who are even less competent in the value-judgment area than their predecessors and who are major contributors to the descending spiral of Hierarchal Regression.

> Cheerful obedience to the computer leads to worse performance by society. It makes it easier for dictators to accomplish their ends. It brings a lessening of freedom. Being loyal to the computer means selling out. . . . The computer is there only to serve man—not to be served by him. —H. MATUSOW

CHAPTER IV

The Mediocracy
or
The Rise and Fall

If fifty million people say a foolish thing, it is
still a foolish thing.

—B. RUSSELL

As Hierarchal Regression increases, the quality of life
retrogresses and viable social institutions degenerate into
giant ineffective self-perpetuating bureaucracies. Everything from products to presidents becomes progressively
less interesting and mediocrity triumphs as the hierarchy
eradicates excellence.

The hierarchy gradually distorts the individual personality so that the citizen may believe he is fulfilling his
personal destiny while in reality he is a programmed
automaton. Nature provides us with an example that is
useful in illustrating this behavior.

The processionary caterpillar is the larvae of the
Cnethocampa processionea and is noted for its style of
advancing along the forest floor. Each processionary caterpillar moves forward with his head abutting the rear end
of his predecessor. As they advance they feed upon oak
leaves, their favorite food. A scientist investigating this
behavior placed a ring of processionary caterpillars around

a flower pot. Each caterpillar had its head abutting the rear end of the one ahead. They proceeded to go round and round the pot until they died of starvation, and yet nearby was their favorite food—oak leaves. The processionary behavior of the caterpillars was not adaptive. Therefore they perished when the solution to their problem was right at hand.

> When people are free to do as they please,
> they usually imitate each other.
>
> —E. Hoffer

Humanness is characterized by adaptive behavior, intelligence, and freedom of choice, but Hierarchal Regression has made humanness progressively more difficult. Although man is not driven by an internal instinctual mechanism as is the caterpillar, he exhibits similar behavior. Man's behavior is conditioned or controlled by the hierarchal system in which he lives. Man behaves more like a puppet than like a caterpillar. A puppet is a figure in the likeness of man whose actions are controlled by external forces. The human victim of Hierarchal Regression could be described as a *Processionary Puppet* who goes through the motions of living, punching cards, filling in forms, and carrying out meaningless rituals.

> Pressed into service means pressed out of shape.
>
> —R. Frost

Today the Processionary Puppet has come into his own as a dynamic social force. He is referred to as the common man, silent majority, mass man, average man, or the consumer.

The Processionary Puppet is a functionary who is impersonal about the content of his work but serious and conscientious about devising new and better bureaucratic procedures. He is deified for his dedication to the means

Man behaves more like a puppet than like a caterpillar.

of his office rather than to its meaning. For example, the astronaut is valued for his efficiency and we take pride in his dramatic exploits in space. The prospect that scientists can put a man on the moon is so cherished by our Processionary Leaders that they tend to turn away from the real problems facing our cities, our country, and our world.

The rise of status of the Processionary Puppet impels man to make an anguished choice. Technical capability provides the power to enable society to solve its problems, but man may fly to the moon while allowing the environment to deteriorate, schools to close, and millions to live in poverty.

> We're about to enter the age of flight, before
> we've even developed a chair that a man can
> sit on comfortably.
>
> —P. WYLIE

The *Professional Processionary Puppet* is defined as the organization man with whom modern society operates its formal organizations. He is a prototype; he has become a symbol of the culture of modern society and he stands for the new élite. Increased specialization has established narrow criteria for success so that promotion within the hierarchy is based on establishmentarian values. This discourages individual potential and submerges human responsibility.

Typically, the Professional Processionary Puppet is a man who begins as a specialist and uses his expertise to win promotions through demonstrating achievement in work for which he is objectively and impersonally qualified. The irony is that the man who does superbly well in his line of work is rewarded by being compelled to leave it, to move up into a higher level of entrapment. This is precisely how a Professional Processionary Puppet is recruited. He is characterized by his lack of responsibility for making policy—he merely carries it out.

> Who is more foolish, the child afraid of the
> dark or the man afraid of the light?
> —M. Freehill

When the Processionary Puppet is in charge, social ends get defined in terms of the socially established means available for their realization. He says, "It can be done, so let's do it." He explores space because the necessary technology exists. He produces nuclear weapons that could overkill the population of the world. He produces hundreds of canisters of germs, each capable of killing a billion persons, and forgets that there are only three billion persons available as potential victims. Why? Because he is a departmentalist who suffers from parochialism, mental inhibition, emotional sterility, and hardening of the categories. He provides no solution to such prob-

lems because solutions concern responsible and humanistic values. He is not involved in the choice between
guns and butter or the choice between rapid-transit systems benefiting millions of citizens and spending thirty
billion dollars to put a man on the moon.

> Where all think alike, no one thinks very much.
> —W. LIPPMANN

Specialization creates expertise of the irresponsible
follow-the-leader type, that in turn must be guided by
layer upon layer of management specialists. Specialization creates the need for bureaucracy. Bureaucracy fosters
an ever more institutionalized and thoroughgoing rule by
mediocrity.

Most high-ranking military men play the Processionary
Puppet role to the hilt. They become heroes by expanding
the scope of their particular function. If questions are
asked about substantive overkill or escalation of wars
against peasant people, the Processionary Puppet is quite
sincere in his answer—"But that is not my department."

The technical expert may become so conforming that
he evolves into an Adolf Eichmann,* a competent Professional Processionary Puppet who can carry us quietly
to destruction. He may become a lobotomized humanoid
whose existence begins and ends with his job. Fortunately,
the extreme cases are still a minority, but none of us can
completely escape the processionary effect.

At present Hierarchal Regression affects all major institutions and contributes to the widespread indifference
to increasing corruption within social institutions. Hierarchal Regression contributes to the descending spiral of
disintegration of the social fabric of civilization and the
general atmosphere of anxiety. Many individuals have

---

* An actual functionary who dutifully carried out the policy
formulated by his government.

become Processionary Puppets and show little anxiety, but those who are concerned about Hierarchal Regression and loss of self suffer because of their awareness. These misfits cry out for change while the silent majority acquires processionary behavior and accepts mediocrity in ethics, education, law, products, and government. Loss of self contributes to acceptance of mediocrity, which then becomes the desired standard. A society ruled by mediocrity is a *Mediocracy* and as such thrives through being operated by Processionary Puppets.

> Mediocrity is merit to the mediocre.
> —J. JOUBERT

The ideal Processionary Puppet is a functionary who has been systematically stripped of his imagination, his creativity, his heritage, his dreams, and his personal uniqueness. Beginning in the public school, if not before, he is conditioned to deal with life by fractionalization of knowledge into compartmentalized academic courses. In this way he is prepared for his mechanistic role in the Mediocracy. As he is drawn into the Mediocracy, overwhelming forces repress honest expressions of feeling and spontaneity. Later, various aspects of his depersonalized, mechanistic job contribute to his further loss of self and his only satisfaction is in ritualistically conforming to his processionary role.

> The English instinctively admire any man who
> has no talent and is modest about it.
> —J. AGATE

In a Mediocracy mass man is served by mass means, which inevitably dictate a general regression of taste and a retreat from excellence. As a consumer the Processionary Puppet becomes an anonymous standardized unit to be serviced. He is a statistic contributing to the general

*The English instinctively admire any man who has
no talent and is modest about it.*

leveling of taste. He is a component of mass culture, mass
traffic, mass fads, mass morality, and mass government.
Technology creates a depersonalized standardized society
which has its effect on the Processionary Puppet by re-
lieving him of responsibility. It frees him from the need
to make decisions. It makes him feel secure as long as
he maintains his processionary behavior. He is a victim
of the Mediocracy and a contributor to its survival as a
social system by becoming a standardized consumer of
products, propaganda, and politics.

> PRICE'S FIRST LAW: If everybody doesn't want
> it, nobody gets it.
>
> —R. PRICE

Bureaus, divisions, and departments within the administrative structure of the Mediocracy tend to become
self-perpetuating, functionary-operated, processionary or-

64   *The Peter Prescription*

ganizations contributing heavily to bureaucratic pollution. Rules, regulations, laws, and bylaws control the individual and invade more and more aspects of his life.

> LES MISERABLES METALAW: * All laws, whether good, bad, or indifferent, must be obeyed to the letter.

A pathological psychological condition develops in the employee within the bureaucratic structure of the Mediocracy. His security depends increasingly on the rules, regulations, rituals, and records of his particular office and he begins to exhibit a senseless, stereotyped, and often vicious kind of institutional paranoia. Internal bureaucratic organizational structures, procedures, and forms are valued more highly than output or public service. The pressure of the Mediocracy upon the official is to be methodical, prudent, and cautious in protecting the rituals of the bureaucracy. He adheres to formal officialdom and punctilious conformity to the ritualistic procedures. His primary concern with conformity to the rules interferes with his producing output or providing service to the public. The chronic Processionary Puppet never forgets a single rule and regards the public as a disruptive force that is motivated to upset the system and get something done.

> Government Bureaucrats are by nature sluggish, secretive, and suspicious—the three S's of their craft.
>
> —B. ATKINSON

Bureaucrats may rise within the hierarchy as a result of negative characteristics. Competence is assessed in terms of not breaking the rules and not causing waves. Where this condition prevails the superior is merely a

---

* A metalaw is a law about laws.

figurehead and it is difficult to distinguish between the
behavior of a leader or a follower.

> When I was a boy, I was told anybody could
> become President; I'm beginning to believe it.
> —C. DARROW

Where this ritualistic behavior occurs within a hierarchy each Processionary Puppet tends to mind his own
business and not to exceed his authority. He may pursue
his assigned task diligently while regression and corruption destroy his department, his company, his society, his
nation.

> All that is necessary for the triumph of evil
> is that good men do nothing.
> —E. BURKE

The Processionary Puppet values belonging. At the
great mass level he takes extraordinary pride in his na-
tionality, religion, or belonging to the majority. At middle-
management levels he belongs to mass organizations,
business clubs, and fraternal societies. At top-management
levels he may prefer membership in private clubs and
exclusive organizations.

> OESER'S LAW: There is a tendency for the per-
> son in the most powerful position in an organi-
> zation to spend all his time serving on commit-
> tees and signing letters.

The ultimate in Hierarchal Regression is the Mediocracy in which the political leadership is derived from
selling to the Processionary Puppet a leader conceived
in his own image. This is achieved through utilization of
the same technology that is employed in mass producing,
packaging, and selling a vast array of products.

> I've got to follow them, I am their leader.
> —LEDRU-ROLLIN

Richard Nixon,* as Presidential candidate, established a new record as the most carefully packaged politician of all time. Opinion polls were conducted and the information collected was processed by computers. This provided public-relations men with the basis for composing statements that the voters wanted to hear. Richard Nixon presented these statements in a series of television commercials directed back to the people who said they wanted to hear them. This is the most proficient selling technique yet devised. Find out what the customer wants and then tell him that is what your package contains. In all fairness to both products and politicians I must remind you that the best to the worst have been sold successfully by this method. The method sells the image, the package, the brand name, and not the contents. It is interesting to note that Hubert H. Humphrey * did not criticize the method employed by his opponent.

> The biggest mistake in my political life was not
> to learn how to use television.
>   —H. HUMPHREY

The Processionary Puppet has been systematically programmed as a consumer. He believes that a vast technology is constantly striving to provide him with new and improved products. It sells him soap that is guaranteed to be superior to any other wash-day product. It then sells him special additives in a variety of colors and forms, granules, liquids, and tablets. Next, it sells him Extra Added Ingredients and New Formulas. It then sells him presoaks to use as a prelude to the washing process and conditioners to add after the process. The Processionary Puppet is convinced that great progress is being made. He is fascinated by changes in the chrome

* Not a fictitious name.

ornaments on his automobile, refrigerator, or other appliances. As a consumer he feels that he is a participant in
progress. He identifies with great events and takes pride
in achievements such as color television or the space program, although he has had no involvement in their
achievement and no real understanding of either. After
a steady diet of TV pap the Processionary Puppet is prepared to accept the packaged politician as something
worthwhile.

> KITMAN'S LAW: Pure drivel tends to drive off
> the TV screen ordinary drivel.
>
> —M. KITMAN

Unfortunately the Packaged Processionary Politician
will most likely be a reflection of the values of the Processionary Puppet, who is a product of Hierarchal Regression; and so the descending spiral is now complete,
from the lowest functionary to the highest office in the
land.

In a well-developed Mediocracy there is no real leader.
The nominal leader is the ultimate follower. The opinion
polls and computers program his behavior. If a fickle
populace expects New Formulas and Extra Added Ingredients as it has been conditioned to expect in other products, then why not in its leaders? The polls indicate that
a man of the people is wanted and so the President is
shown at his barbecue pit, watching TV, petting his dog,
or playing golf. When the people tire of the old image
they are shown the new President, and then the new,
new President, and then the new, new, new President,
with his new hair style, new rhetoric, new image, and
new slogan.

> I do not know upon what subject he will next
> employ his versatile incapacity.
>
> —A. HOUSMAN

Even though the Peter Principle operates not only to bring the individual to his level of incompetence and also ultimately to erode the fabric of the entire society, each of us can become more creative, confident, and competent. By so doing we will not only save ourselves from personal incompetence but will also contribute to reversing the Hierarchal Regression that is destroying society.

> The true test of a civilization is not the census, nor the size of cities, nor the crops—no, but the kind of man the country turns out.
>
> —R. W. Emerson

The opposite end of the human spectrum from the Processionary Puppet is the *Humanite*. A Humanite has qualities of humanness including mental cultivation, benevolence, and self-actualization. A Humanite is a human being who fulfills his potential and derives satisfaction from being creative, confident, and competent.

> Every man has in himself a continent of undiscovered character. Happy he who acts the Columbus to his own soul!
>
> —J. Stephen

PART TWO

Protect Your Competence

Reason's whole pleasure, all the joys of sense,
be in three words: health, peace, and competence.

—ALEXANDER POPE

CHAPTER V

Know Thyself
or
A Little Introspection
Does You Good!

Life is an endless process of self-discovery.
—J. GARDNER

W HEN the oracle at Delphi said, "Know thyself," she wasn't just speaking Greek, she was saying something for all mankind about the importance of acquiring a sense of identity. Identity is as necessary for survival of your individual integrity as food, clothing, and shelter are for your physical survival.

> The precept "Know Thyself" was not solely intended to obviate the pride of mankind; but likewise that we might understand our own worth.
> —M. T. CICERO

Disaster plagues the man who no longer knows himself, for he has lost his special immunity to a multitude of modern ills. Prostrated in front of a television set and exposed to all manner of lies about himself, he is defenseless against the pressures that envelop him. Seized with

71

guilt about his social position and yearning for security, he joins the status seekers and throws himself into a fit of competition and conformity that lays waste his natural powers.

> The mass of men lead lives of quiet desperation.
>
> —H. Thoreau

Modern man may be aware that he has gone into debt to purchase items he rarely uses. He feels there is something terribly wrong with his life but is reluctant to admit it, although he may discuss his problems in terms of emotional repressions or psychological hangups. He may try to correct these in group sessions, sensitivity training, or private therapy, or he may just blindly try harder and hope for the best.

But when questioned, especially in the presence of his frustrated spouse and rebellious children, he will insist, "I'm doing all right for myself," and will point to his material possessions as proof of his success. He has become a Processionary Puppet.

Social scientists have been warning us for decades about the dehumanizing effect of our production-oriented society. Philosophers throughout the ages have urged us to heed the message, know thyself, but they have failed to provide practical instructions so that each of us can achieve that true self-knowledge that yields the power to shape our personal destinies.

A common problem afflicting civilized man is his identity crises. He is confused by the question, Who am I? To some degree this is a problem for all of us within the hierarchy's influence. Your identity is a synthesis of your perception of yourself, your view of your world, and your vision of your ideal life style. With the acquisition of a strong personal identity you will be less vulnerable to psychological disintegration and will establish the foundations for self-esteem.

Your self-esteem is your conviction that you are uniquely valuable and is based on your sense of competence to accomplish something vital to your individuality. When you have achieved self-esteem you will have the capacity to live creatively and make your life your own Humanite project.

> A man has to live with himself, and he should
> see to it that he always has good company.
> —C. E. HUGHES

Creative living frees your imagination to produce solutions to problems and to restructure your life into what you want it to be. You will then listen to your real self and respect your own opinions, uninhibited by inner conflicts and doubts.

> You are not in charge of the universe: you are
> in charge of yourself.
> —A. BENNETT

Right now is the beginning of the rest of your life. Move forward toward more happiness, awareness, aliveness, responsiveness, and fulfillment of your unique Humanite potential.

> Make the most of yourself for that is all there
> is of you.
> —R. W. EMERSON

PETER PRESCRIPTION 1
The Peter Preparation: *Revitalize your body*

The mind and body are in reality an inseparable unity. Their relationship is such that you cannot think clearheadedly about yourself when your body is overcome with fatigue, intoxicants, or illness. A healthy body is an essential prerequisite to the maximum benefits you can derive from the other prescriptions.

> The greatest mistake a man can make is to sacrifice health for any other advantage.
> —A. SCHOPENHAUER

The belief that the mind has good and bad effects on the body is as old as recorded history. Few would dispute the validity of the old belief that "As a man thinketh so is he." Granting the eternal wisdom of old but ever new truths is one thing, but it is also a reality that the body is renewed and revived by food and rest, not by thinking, no matter how noble that thinking is.

Prolonged worry is destructive to all organs of the body and interferes with the digestion and assimilation of even the best of food. Although destructive emotions impair both clear thinking and bodily function, many individuals have found to their lasting satisfaction that revitalizing their bodies has produced unexpected rewards of tranquillity and joy.

> Health alone is victory.
> —T. CARLYLE

To know thyself you must know your body. You achieved your present physical state as a result of millions of years of human development. Your body evolved through adaptations to a wide variety of environmental conditions. The recent accelerated escalation of environmental change has not given your body time to adapt. Your muscles and circulatory system were not designed for a life of inactivity and your digestive system was not intended to function on a diet of refined and imitation foods, devoid of nutrition and inundated with preservatives. Over a period of future generations man's body, if it can survive the shocks of rapid change, may adapt to inactivity and to chemically fertilized food crops polluted with insecticides and other poisons.

Our bodies are apt to be our autobiographies.
—F. BURGESS

Every cell and organ of your body tends to increase in function through regular exercise. The health of your cells and organs depends upon rich healthy blood, actively distributed throughout your body by heart, muscle, arteries, and capillaries. Daily vigorous exercise is an important ingredient in the revitalization of your body and the maintenance of your health. Bicycling, swimming, hiking, jogging, gardening, exercise, and games can be alternated to provide a variety of activities that will

Daily vigorous exercise is an important ingredient.

enrich your life while improving your respiration, increasing your circulation, and toning up your body.

Your body cannot be better than the food used each day to nourish, strengthen, and rebuild it. The blood that supplies the vital source for your every cell, tissue, and organ is nourished with good food, air, and water. Fortunately, today there is a renewed interest in natural food as the source of vitamins, minerals, and other nutritive elements that vitalize our bodies and provide resistance to disease.

Through early detection of abnormalities, by periodic check-ups with your physician, and improved medical treatment, you can avoid many serious illnesses. By combining adequate medical care with your own program for revitalization of your body, constructive thinking, cheerfulness, and peace of mind will ensue.

> Health is the thing that makes you feel that
> now is the best time of the year.
> —F. P. ADAMS

PETER PRESCRIPTION 2
The Peter Peacemaker: *Take a vacation every day*

This is a simple mental exercise that will take you away from your worldly cares and put you in special communion with your inner self. It is not an original discovery on my part—people have been doing it for centuries and have called it by many different names. Anyone can do it.

To perform the Peter Peacemaker you must totally relax your body, close your eyes, and clear your mind of all distracting thought. Then, gently seek out that peaceful center within yourself where all is very quiet and beautiful. At first you may require some time and effort to find it, but with practice you will soon be able to close your eyes and immediately be there.

If you are inexperienced in relaxation techniques, begin by sitting in a comfortable chair with your feet on the floor and your hands resting easily in your lap. Close your eyes and breathe evenly, deeply, and gently. As you exhale each breath let your body become more relaxed. Starting with one hand direct your attention to one part of your body at a time. Close your fist and tighten the muscles in your forearm. Feel the sensation of tension in your muscles. Relax your hand and let your forearm and hand become completely limp. Direct all your attention to the sensation of relaxation as you continue to let all tension leave your hand and arm. Continue this practice once or several times each day, relaxing your other hand and arm, your legs, back, abdomen, chest, neck, face, and scalp. When you have this mastered and can relax completely, turn your thoughts to scenes of peaceful beauty. Begin, if you wish, by recalling pleasant scenes of natural tranquillity from your past. Stay with your inner self as long as you wish, either thinking of nothing or visualizing only the loveliest of images. Often you will become completely unaware of your surroundings. When you open your eyes you will find yourself refreshed in mind and body.

Those who practice the Peter Peacemaker say it has changed their lives. Not only has it helped them to unwind, break obsessional thought patterns, and fall asleep more easily, but it has also taught them to accept and enjoy their moods instead of fighting them. As one of my students put it, "Blues come and go, but that calm place inside of me always remains."

> To have a quiet mind is to possess one's mind wholly; to have a calm spirit is to command one's self.
>
> —H. Mabie

E. Z. Ryder is a supermarket manager who lives with his wife and two children in a house on the edge of town.

Every morning after he boards the bus for work, E. Z. closes his eyes and retreats into a peaceful place inside his mind. By the time he has reached his destination, he is ready to begin his day with the calmness that has carried over from his restful retreat. E. Z. sometimes repeats this exercise during the day, especially if he has a particularly hectic schedule. He has found that it allows him to make more rational decisions. E. Z. is well known for his presence of mind in times of crisis.

Recently an acquaintance noticed E. Z. sitting quietly by himself. He inquired if anything was the matter.

"Nothing's the matter," E. Z. replied with a smile. "It's just that sometimes happiness is quiet."

> Each one has to find his peace from within, and peace to be real must be unaffected by outside circumstances.   —M. GANDHI

PETER PRESCRIPTION 3
The Peter Panorama: *List your most satisfying activities*

This prescription has helped many healthy individuals find greater joy in their lives and it has assisted many disturbed and confused persons find solutions to their problems. One advantage to making lists is that it is cheaper than psychotherapy and you can pin your list on the wall and reflect on it. You cannot do this to your psychiatrist.

Your first list should include the things you like about your life—joyful experiences, pleasant reminiscences, anything that has produced a sense of satisfaction. The most common difficulty in making this list is the error of including things that you thought would be satisfying but actually turned out to be unrewarding. The boat you pur-

Make a list of your most satisfying activities.

chased that required more maintenance and imposed more responsibility than it provided pleasure, the expensive entertainment that was boring, or the prestigious social event where you actually felt uncomfortable are examples of the things that may originally appear on your list. After consideration cross these off. Think about all aspects of your existence—material possessions, love, work, play. Add to your list over a period of a few days as you recall your happy times.

When you feel that your list is reasonably complete, go over it several times and mark those items that you could repeat daily or at least fairly regularly. Now write these on a second list. Excluded from this list will be items that have periodic limitations, such as opening presents on Christmas and graduating from school. You should also exclude those events which are a matter of beautiful dumb luck, such as being dealt a royal flush or drawing a winning ticket in a lottery. Your second list should include the things you can do, such as making love, cooking, sailing, painting, gardening, playing chess, golfing, and so forth.

The first list will provide you with plenty of material for introspection about the range of things that make you happy; but the second list will become your faithful companion. Look at the second list every day and you will become increasingly aware of the ways your daily life can be more satisfying. You will find yourself doing more of these things. Do not be discouraged if the results are not immediate. Continue to go over your list and find time regularly for some of the more satisfying activities. Do not be hesitant to add new items to your list—you can always cross them off if they fail to produce the expected results.

What will all this do for you besides make your days somewhat more pleasant? It turns out that those who carry out this prescription over a long period of time discover that large areas of their lives begin to change. With only so many hours during the day, the enjoyable events begin to crowd out the neutral, unpleasant, and irrelevant. Sometimes, even an ingrained life style will give way under the force of a multitude of pleasant and satisfying happenings.

> Happiness is not a station you arrive at, but a manner of traveling.
>
> —M. RUNBECK

PETER PRESCRIPTION 4
The Peter Purification: *Rid your life of the ghosts of the past*

It is possible to spend an enormous amount of time and energy worrying and projecting imaginary miseries into the future. The worrier contaminates his present activities with apprehensions. He lives in a psychological nether world. Remembrances of his mistakes, misunderstandings, and tragedies inhibit his mind. His memories tell him, "You are a product of your parents, your environment, your society—you are your past." The worrier feels doomed to a life of backing reluctantly into the present with his eyes fixed firmly on the past. His thoughts allow him no peace and are inconsiderate of his digestion, sleep, and sex life.

If you are a worrier, bury your mistakes by substituting positive behavior in the present. Assure yourself that you are not going to repeat your mistakes willfully. Your task is to live effectively in the here and now. The Peter Prescriptions will help you do this by providing positive substitute modes of behavior that will reduce your worry habit.

> I tell you the past is a bucket of ashes.
> —C. SANDBURG

PETER PRESCRIPTION 5
The Peter Pimpernel: *Be your own hero*

Make your life an adventure in which you are proud of your role. A hero acts nobly of his own free will, either in opposition to or beyond what is expected of him. To be your own hero, seek out your inner strengths and use them creatively. Decide what qualities you think a hero possesses. Is a hero someone who stands up for what he believes? You can do that. Is he someone who works patiently toward a significant goal? You can do that, too.

Explore your abilities and beliefs. Remember—every time you act originally and decisively you reaffirm your identity, increase your self-esteem, and become your own hero.

The smoker who feels that he is a victim of his addiction will be his own hero when he has kicked the habit.

The homemaker who consciously avoids using detergents that are polluters and who stops contributing to the escalation of the throwaway society becomes her own heroine.

> Heroes in history seem to us poetic because they are there. But if we should tell the simple truth of some of our neighbors, it would sound like poetry.
>
> —G. CURTIS

Occasionally by simply taking an effective stand for his rights, an individual may also become a public hero. V. Hickle bought a new car that immediately broke down because of defective parts. When his local dealer refused to replace the car, Hickle painted a huge yellow lemon on its side and parked it in front of the dealer's office. Hickle's unusual deed gave him an intense feeling of pride, national attention, and eventually a satisfactory new car.

> The best reformers the world has ever seen are those who commence on themselves.
>
> —G. B. SHAW

PETER PRESCRIPTION 6
The Peter Pride: *Reward yourself for what you do*

Everyone needs approval. Approval is one of the strongest rewards or reinforcements. The hierarchy has developed processionary behavior that depends excessively on the approval of others.

Self-evaluation and self-reward produce a shift from being other-directed to being inner-directed. Individuals who do not learn to reinforce themselves endlessly seek approval from others and become the victims of unsatisfying escalation.

To protect your individuality from the eroding influences of a hectic, frustrating world, regularly take time out for self-reward. This connects you to your actions and provides enduring satisfaction. Besides, the rewards of others are empty without your own self-regard to back them up.

The Peter Pride differs from general self-adulation and positive wishful-thinking approaches. It is a specific prescription that requires you to evaluate your own performance in relation to your objectives and the Humanite qualities you wish to strengthen. If your evaluation of your behavior shows you are being consistent with the qualities you desire, then tell yourself, "I certainly handled the situation well!" or "That was a constructive idea I came up with." Your mind will be stimulated by this sort of internal commentary. As you practice self-evaluation and self-reward, you will strengthen your identity and be less vulnerable to the effects of unwarranted criticism.

> The advantage of doing one's praising for oneself is that one can lay it on so thick and exactly in the right places.
>
> —S. BUTLER

PETER PRESCRIPTION 7
The Peter Pragmatic: *Do things for others*

"Pragmatic" means springing from experience rather than from theory—practical experience is the basis of this prescription. It is common experience for one to find his identity while helping others or at least to discover some new things about himself while giving of himself.

The Peter Pragmatic is not in conflict with the other prescriptions for facilitating your individual identity; rather it prescribes your voluntary decision to do something for others where the only reward that you foresee is probable Peter Pride. If your self-esteem and satisfaction are enhanced when you help someone, start a humanitarian enterprise, or contribute to a cause you consider worthwhile, you have discovered something important about yourself.

The Peter Pragmatic must not be confused with doing something for the establishment hierarchy where the rewards of external approval, prestige, or gain are predictable.

> The service we render to others is really the
> rent we pay for our room on this earth.
> —W. GRENFELL

A great deal of Peter Pride can be derived from voluntarily giving of oneself. It is your proof that you have achieved the degree of identity that determines who you are, what you are, and what you can do. When you can give without feeling that you need appreciation from the receiver or approval from society, you have achieved your identity as a Humanite.

> Avarice and happiness never saw each other,
> how then should they become acquainted?
> —B. FRANKLIN

PETER PRESCRIPTION 8
The Peter Pledge: *Reaffirm your belief in yourself*

The Peter Pledge is a reminder of what I have learned about living a personally rewarding life. Any personal pledge, repeated regularly, will provide you with a valuable reorientation in what is often a very disorienting world. You can write your own pledge or use mine or someone else's. The origin of the wording does not matter as long as the pledge supports your identity and Humanite values.

> As a member in good standing of the Family of Man,
> I pledge to respect myself and others and express in word and action the regard I feel.
> I pledge that each act and decision will be forward to a better-quality life, and not upward to incompetence.
> I pledge that I will keep in touch with myself.
> —L. PETER

CHAPTER VI

Know Thy Hierarchy
or
Up the Ladder

Whom the gods wish to destroy they first call
promising.
—C. CONNOLLY

Up to this point in our discussion, hierarchies have been
viewed simplistically. Now, as an advanced student of
hierarchiology, you are ready for an in-depth study of
hierarchal systems.

Life is now in session. Are you present?
—B. COPELAND

Hierarchal escalation has been described in layman language as "climbing the ladder of success," or "up the
establishment ladder." The common use of a ladder as an
analogy for the hierarchy has led to a general misunder-
standing of the nature of hierarchies. A ladder has certain
characteristics that are common to a hierarchy. For example, a ladder is used for climbing upward and the
higher you climb the greater the danger. Hierarchies are
unlike most ladders in three fundamental ways: (1) the
step size, or distance between one rung and the next,
varies; (2) the rungs are movable; and (3) eligibility to
take a step is determined by a number of different systems
of promotion.

Dow's LAW: In a hierarchical organization, the
higher the level, the greater the confusion.

1. Step Size

The education hierarchy most closely resembles a ladder. The intellectually competent child will most likely spend one year in each grade. Only rarely will he be allowed to skip and if he does he will skip the standard step—one school year. Similarly, when a child fails, he repeats one school year.

Although the step size established by the educational hierarchy appears to be uniformly one school year, in actual operation one step may be more difficult than another. A child endowed with superior intellect and a favorable environment may climb the educational ladder step by step with comparative ease. A less fortunate child may struggle hard, repeat grades, and end up dropping out of school because some of the steps were too difficult. Step variations of this type exist in every hierarchy. The ability to navigate one step does not assure success in reaching the next.

Another aspect of step size is the actual distance between the rungs. The average student who is punctual, obedient, and dependable and who completes assignments as prescribed has little difficulty in public school or college. If the student then attempts graduate school he may be in for a surprise. Graduate schools in some universities still believe that sixteen or more years of conforming scholarship prepare a student to be a creative scientist. Where this unrealistic expectation exists, the undergraduate moving to graduate school must manage an educational step of unprecedented size and may find himself suddenly at his level of incompetence. Fortunately for graduates at most universities, this step has been reduced and graduate work is simply a continuation of conforming

The average student has little difficulty in public school.

educational consumerism, terminated by a thesis that is
merely a statistical validation of a creative discovery made
by an independent scholar from the past.

> The average Ph.D. thesis is nothing but a
> transference of bones from one graveyard to
> another.
>
> —J. FRANK DOBIE

The individual in any organization may find himself at
a level of incompetence when the promotion consists of
an unusually large step. A man of modest means, managing his finances reasonably well, may prove to be financially incompetent upon inheriting great wealth. The
competent within a military or political hierarchy may
achieve sudden incompetence when promoted from follower to leader. The competent scientist may become an
incompetent administrator when promoted to research
director. Each of these promotions produces sudden incompetence because it demands new abilities that were

not required during the individual's preceding escalations.

A promotee may achieve maximum incompetence gradually through several promotions. An employee producing quality work may be promoted to a supervisory position where he is moderately competent. In time he may gain a management-level position in which he is only marginally incompetent. This may be as far up the ladder as he will go, but, if other hierarchal conditions are favorable, he may be able to achieve maximum incompetence. As a marginally incompetent incumbent he requires vast amounts of time to complete routine tasks. If he is provided with additional competent subordinates, he may be able to produce adequate output. As a marginally incompetent manager he can be supported by a competent staff. Because he still appears competent and now has the additional prestige of heading a large staff, he may receive a further promotion. As general manager his chief responsibility is for decisions affecting broad corporate goals and policies. He has now achieved maximum incompetence. He became progressively less competent as he moved from doing quality work to positions dealing with broader goals and higher levels of abstraction.

Many reports received have described how an employee first appeared incompetent following a promotion, but in time became competent. My investigations disclosed that this was in fact rare. In most cases the incompetent promotee was protected by his superiors who wanted their promotional decision to look good. Competent subordinates were assigned to assist the promotee and difficult jobs were delegated to other employees or departments. In time the position was whittled down to a size the promotee could handle—"he had grown into the job."

The first and worst of all frauds is to cheat oneself. All sin is easy after that.   —J. BAILEY

Educational, political, and military hierarchies are primarily pyramidal structures based upon the Peter Principle, where an individual enters at the bottom and climbs to his level. Even within these hierarchies prejudices and restrictions exist that prevent or impede members of certain groups from reaching the top. In the military, for example, chaplains, medical doctors, and women have had limited opportunities to become field commanders. In politics, women, intellectuals, and blacks have not had equal opportunities for nomination to high office as have members of other groups.

Professional barriers also create hierarchal complexities. In a hospital the medical doctors form one hierarchy, while technicians, administrators, nurses, service, and maintenance personnel each form their own. The most competent sweeper is not promoted to become a nurse or doctor unless he engages in extensive retraining to change his profession. In other situations, changing from hierarchy to hierarchy or profession to profession is quite easy. A lawyer, soldier, businessman, or actor can become a politician without undergoing professional retraining.

Knowledge of these characteristics of step size provides you with flexibility in your hierarchal maneuvers.

> Knowledge is power.
> —F. Bacon

2. The Movable Rung

We are saddened to see the passing of old and honored trades. The carriage builder, the village blacksmith, the wheelwright, and the buggy-whip maker became irrelevant as a result of technological change. The apprentice entering one of these trades during the era of the automobile take-over found that by the time he had achieved his master-craftsman status, the rung he had climbed to had moved and in some cases disappeared.

In recent times automation and the computer have reduced the status of some jobs, eliminated others, and created a whole new hierarchy of data processers. If we are going to use the ladder analogy, then we must visualize a ladder in which rungs are moved up and down, rungs are removed, and rungs are added.

> Nought endures but change.
> —L. BOURNE

D. Deadend was frustrated because he had difficulty obtaining steady employment. He visited T. Middlegroove, the vocational counselor at Excelsior Vocational School, who explained that Deadend failed because of his low academic achievement and that he had not acquired any salable skills. He recommended that Deadend enroll in a shoe-repairing course. Deadend told his friends, "At last I am learning a trade. My future will be secure."

Deadend was dexterous and persevering and graduated from the course. When he looked for work he reported, "I can't find a job anywhere. Shoe repairing is a dying trade. Excelsior City shops are folding. It's only the old people who have their shoes repaired—the young people throw them away and buy new ones." Deadend had climbed to a disappearing rung.

> Life is like an onion: you peel it off one layer
> at a time, and sometimes you weep.
> —C. SANDBURG

In the marital hierarchy, most wives have already been relieved of such duties as milking cows, churning butter, stoking fires, making quilts, and preserving food. Many are now free of broom pushing, mop swinging, vegetable peeling, and bread baking. Television has become a combined babysitter and storyteller. The modern wife is expected to function at a higher level. As the rung is moved up, she becomes the family economist, child psychologist, and career woman. Many women who would have been competent wives in an earlier era reach their level of incompetence on this higher rung.

Few husbands now have to turn their hands to such old chores as clearing land, harnessing horses, cutting wood, tending beehives, and cultivating crops. The present-day husband is on a rung requiring sophisticated managerial, diplomatic, financial, and love-making competence. So we see that marriages are more likely to collapse now than they were when the marital hierarchy had many more steps.

> Marriage is a lottery, but you can't tear up
> your ticket if you lose.
>
> —F. KNOWLES

The movable rung has two main effects on the hierarchy: (1) As rungs disappear from the *bottom* of a hierarchy, the probability increases that for any new recruit, the initial placement will be his final placement; and (2) as rungs are taken away from the *middle* of a hierarchy, the gaps between the remaining rungs grow wider. As each promotional step becomes larger, the transition from former to new duties becomes more difficult, resulting in an increased probability that any promotion will be to a level of incompetence.

> Success is full of promise till men get it: and
> then it is a last-year's nest from which the birds
> have flown.
>
> —H. BEECHER

3. Systems of Promotion

In feudal times man was content to live within a non-promotion system and remain at a level of competence for a lifetime.

God bless the Squire and his relations
And keep us in our proper stations.
—OLD PRAYER

Modern hierarchal systems make replacements from below to fill vacancies caused by promotions higher up, resignations, retirements, dismissals, and deaths. There is also a tendency to make more promotions than the minimum in an attempt to increase efficiency (if three vice presidents are useful, six must be better) and as an incentive to keep employees happy (if Maude Lynne can get promoted, there must be hope for me).

Let us then be up and doing with a heart for
any fate.
—H. LONGFELLOW

PROMOTION BY OUTPUT In organizations employing performance standards stated as measurable objectives, it is possible to promote an employee on the basis of how well he achieves these stated goals. In this situation *competence* is defined as *the performance of a job in a way which produces the desired output*. This system is not widely used because defining objectives and evaluating performance are difficult tasks.

It is better to be a nobody who accomplishes
something than a somebody who accomplishes
nothing.
—A. PUNDIT

PROMOTION BY INPUT When an employee is appreciated for his punctuality, neatness, obedience to the rules and rituals, agreeing with the boss and laughing at his jokes, having a smiling face turned upward to his superiors, and playing office politics, he is valued for his input. In this situation *competence* is defined as *contributing to the smooth internal functioning of the organization*.

> Ambition often puts men upon doing the mean-
> est offices: so climbing is performed in the same
> posture with creeping.
>
> —J. SWIFT

PROMOTION BY PREFERENCE There are two major classifications of preference promotions—stereotype preference
and secret preference. In stereotype preference the characteristics that constitute competence are well known and
may even be published as a personnel policy statement.
Some companies will not promote a fat man while others
will only promote those who dress in a company-approved
style. In this situation *competence* is defined as *conformity
to the company stereotype.*

Secret preference is based on the personal likes, dislikes,
and hidden values of those in power. For example, J. Mandible, president of Mandible Alligator Bags, hired his
son-in-law, A. Wedman, as office manager. T. Nightingale,
a tenor in Mandible's church choir, was promoted from
stockboy in the raw-alligator-hide department to assistant
shipper. J. Treadright, who actively supported the political
candidate favored by Mandible, was promoted from wire
bender in the frame shop to foreman. These promotions
were by secret preference because nowhere was it stated
that promotions were based on whom you married, where
you sang, or how you voted. In this situation *competence*
is defined as *the ability to discover and cater to the superior's personal preferences.*

> Power tends to corrupt; absolute power cor-
> rupts absolutely.   —LORD ACTON

PROMOTION BY SENIORITY Unions and other professional
organizations have supported the seniority system in an
effort to counteract the unfairness of preference promotions. Early attempts to use the system in its pure form
had serious repercussions.

Around the turn of the century members of the Excelsior Fire Department were hired, promoted, and fired according to preference of the City Fathers. The Local of the Anti-Combustion Workers' and Ladder Scalers' International demanded and obtained job security and seniority rights. Three months later the Fire Chief reached the age of sixty-five and, as departmental rules prescribed, immediately retired.

The Deputy Chief had been groomed for the Chief's job and had naturally expected the promotion, but under the new seniority rules the Deputy, the four Zone Commanders, and all the Captains, Lieutenants, and Squad Leaders were passed over in favor of J. Doddring, who, two weeks short of his sixty-fifth birthday, was the senior member of the Department.

The Deputy Chief resigned in a huff and his post was filled by Stan Patt, another rank-and-file fireman who was Doddring's junior by three days, before compulsory retirement. With 420 men in the Department, serving an average term of thirty-five years from recruitment to retirement, the average tenure of the Chief's office became one month, with a similar rapid turnover in all ranks.

By the rules of the Excelsior Fire Department and similar seniority systems, *competence* is defined as *the ability to survive*.

Where promotion goes by seniority the characteristic attitude of employees is caution: "Never take a risk!" "Play it safe!" "Let George do it!" Combined with this lack of enterprise is a high degree of contentment because under this system everyone can become Chief.

Excelsior City briefly experienced a slight reduction in the cost of operating its Fire Department. The new cautious attitude of the firemen resulted in fewer injuries and a consequent decline in workmen's compensation payments. The firemen's ultra-cautious attitude reduced their efficiency in extinguishing fires. Fire-insurance rates in Excelsior City rose sharply.

For the above reasons the seniority system is seldom used in its pure state.

> Traditionalists are pessimistic about the future
> and optimists about the past.
>
> —L. MUMFORD

PROMOTION BY PARTICIPATIVE SELECTION In the examples presented so far, it appears that promotion is authoritative, that is, the selection always comes from above. This, of course, is not strictly true. Frequently the prospective promotee is consulted regarding his feelings about the promotion. Although he may participate in the decision, for the promotion to become effective it must have the superior's approval. Most modern management experts condemn authoritative and extol the virtues of participative management. This appears to be based on the unwarranted assumption that the promotee will be able to identify his own competence level. *Competence* in the participative-selection system is defined as *the prospective promotee's ability to assess his own performance with an adequate degree of objectivity.*

> An idealist is one who, on noticing that a rose
> smells better than a cabbage, concludes that it
> will also make better soup.
>
> —H. MENCKEN

The Peter Pain and Pleasure Process

The questions I am asked most frequently are: "Why does man keep struggling onward and upward when, if he would stop climbing, there is much to enjoy?" "Why is man so competitive?" "Why does man accept every challenge to escalate his power, to own a second car, boat, and vacation home, to build a bigger bomb and to fly to the moon?" The answer to these questions is found in simple learning principles.

When a behavior produces a reward or satisfaction, that behavior will tend to increase in the future. When a behavior produces pain or discomfort, that behavior will tend to decrease in the future. This process is the basis of all learning, from the simplest of animal training to the highest level of rational or scientific thought.

As long as behavior is responsive to the *Peter Pain and Pleasure Process*, that behavior is adaptive and will support the survival of the organism emitting the behavior. Unresponsiveness results when the behavior becomes autonomous or internalized so that it persists in spite of its destructive consequences.

> The real question of physical and moral health in man as well as in animals is how well he is able to do his work and enjoy his life, and how fit he is yet to survive.
>
> —LIN YUTANG

Let us examine what happens as civilized man's hierarchies become entrenched.

The infant is born into a family that is competitive with other family units. The child's parents may try to outdo other parents in providing their child with better toys, clothes, or sports equipment, or they may compete in the provision of prestigious nursery schooling or pediatric, orthodontic, or psychiatric care. The child's success in toilet training, walking, and early schooling all bring forth his parents' expressions of appreciation, adoration, and love.

Up until the beginning of his formal schooling the child learns that he is a consumer and that receiving toys, clothes, food, and entertainment are associated with smiles, cuddles, and approval. He learns that his value is related to the acquisition of possessions. He also learns that his value is related to his achievements.

School offers a completely systematized application of the Peter Pain and Pleasure Process in the acquisition of escalationary behavior. Each assignment is carefully graded so that the child knows exactly how much approval his performance has been awarded. His status with his teacher, classmates, and family is contingent upon his achievement in school. The school itself is the perfect hierarchy. The student's competence in first grade is his eligibility to second grade and so on, until he escapes out the top with his university degree or laterally when he reaches his level of incompetence.

During his formative years in the total indoctrination in upward mobility he is consistently rewarded for escalationary behavior—completing assignments, earning high grades, winning awards, and outdoing his classmates in academics, sports, debate, and social activities. Climbing the hierarchal ladder is so consistently reinforced that it becomes internalized and operates as automatic behavior.

> Perhaps the most valuable result of all education is the ability to make yourself do the thing you have to do, when it ought to be done, whether you like it or not. This is the first lesson to be learned.
>
> —T. Huxley

When the graduate enters the world of work he does not leave the influence of home and school behind. Getting a job, gaining promotions, earning raises, improving qualifications—all pay off in terms of satisfaction.

It is appropriate that the behavior described above is commonly called "joining the rat race," because rats can be put on a hierarchal schedule of reinforcement where they will persist in racing mindlessly in an endless competition with their cagemates. Civilized man has built a system of entrapment wherein he continually strives for more and cannot refuse a challenge, however meaningless.

> Like dogs in a wheel, birds in a cage or squirrels in a chain, ambitious men still climb and climb, with great labor and incessant anxiety, but never reach the top.
>
> —H. BURTON

Escalation is not an evil in itself if it serves a survival, safety, aesthetic, or humanitarian purpose. Escalation that leads to hypertension, gastric ulcers, keeping up with the Joneses, acquisition of unused possessions, environmental degradation, and of excessive wealth and power is destructive of the good life.

> It's great to be great, but it's greater to be human.
>
> —W. ROGERS

Our homes, our schools, our total society have trained us in processionary behavior. Unless some other force enters a man's life, he will go struggling ever upward until death, debility, or enforced retirement puts an end to his striving for striving's sake.

> To reach the height of our ambition is like trying to reach the rainbow; as we advance it recedes.
>
> —E. BURKE

The individual viewing this reality rationally may decide to drop out of the rat race and start a new, more rewarding life. Many young people today question the escalation game. They see the older generation as the exemplification of the Peter Principle. This lack of enthusiasm for the establishmentarian hierarchy has resulted in their experimentation with alternate life styles.

> Ours is a world where people don't know what they want and are willing to go through hell to get it.
>
> —D. Marquis

Persons representing many walks of life have discussed with me the moment of truth that brought their rational powers into action. A business executive told me that he had been offered a promotion. He stopped to consider the purpose of his life and as he identified the rewards of the higher office he began to realize the carrot-on-a-stick nature of the system. His perception began to clear and he saw that satisfactions in life were available to him now if he would only reach out from where he was. He cherished and enjoyed his family. He realized that the promotion would mean less time with his children. Providing more money was not the greatest gift he could bestow upon them. He had made the discovery that the art of living was within his reach. He went on to say that his family life was even more rewarding and his peace of mind and health had improved. This man's glowing testimony showed that he had found his own Peter Prescription for avoiding processionary behavior and was moving forward to real Humanite fulfillment.

> Life's greatest achievement is in the continual remaking of yourself so that at last you know how to live.
>
> —W. Rhodes

The Processionary Puppet cannot fight the system that is the source of his reinforcement. His day of independence is over and he feels guilt and shame at the mere hint of arousal of independent thought. Because he considers such thoughts to be disloyal, he represses his individuality and overreacts to others who express criticism of the establishment.

The Humanite cannot function without courage because at times his independently determined values may be in conflict with those of the establishment.

> Its name is Public Opinion. It is held in reverence. It settles everything. Some think it is the voice of God.
>
> —M. TWAIN

Processionary behavior becomes so deeply imbedded that it requires some very powerful rational thinking to counteract it. Persons of a philosophical turn of mind are more likely to come to the realization that continual escalation of wealth and power is no more valid for man than was continual escalation of bulk for the dinosaur or continual escalation of fang for the saber-toothed tiger.

> The spirit of the age is filled with disdain for thinking.
>
> —A. SCHWEITZER

Unfortunately, for most individuals rational powers do not come into action unless they are shocked into doing so. Usually it takes a great personal tragedy to awaken the mind to the real beauty of life. A typical revelation occurs when a man has been struggling up the hierarchy, advancing professionally, gaining status, obtaining possessions, and sudden illness stops him in his tracks. The enforced inactivity sometimes coupled with the threat of death causes him to look to each day for what it offers. He may see the beauty of a sunset, feel the warm concern of those who love him, experience anew the sensual pleasure of the smell of a rose, the taste of honey, or the sound of laughter. He begins to identify the things that are most meaningful in his life—acts of kindness, scenes of beauty, doing things for others. If he recovers he may live the remainder of his life fulfilling the Peter Prescription or he may again succumb gradually to the hierarchal reinforcement system.

> The quality, not the longevity, of one's life is what is important.
>
> —M. L. KING, JR.

The testimony of so many who did not appreciate life until personal tragedy shocked them into thinking has convinced me that our educational and social system is failing to teach us how to think meaningfully about life.

> Cradled and sealed in a human skull,
> Locked in a chamber both dark and dull,
> Weary from wasting the years away
> A mind is lying asleep today.
> Lulled to rest by the teacher's scene
> And the golden glow from the TV screen;
> Reinforced in procession by the world's caress,
> And the steady drone from the ad man's press.
> A puppet loath to face the light,
> Tragedy strikes and shows the right.
> For life on earth there's a better way
> So a mind awakens to the light of day.
>
> —L. PETER

PETER PRESCRIPTION 9
The Peter Profile: *Explore your personal history*

Find a quiet time and place where you can relax and think about the past. Let your mind take you back to your earliest recollection of your feelings of satisfaction when you received approval or other rewards. As you relive these experiences, identify the influences that shaped your escalatory behavior. When you understand how your competitive behavior developed, you will gain more conscious control over it.

> May you live all the days of your life.
> —J. Swift

PETER PRESCRIPTION 10
The Peter Probe: *Examine the satisfiers maintaining your present behavior*

The Peter Pain and Pleasure Process is operating on you whether you are conscious of it or not. By identifying specifically those things that are satisfiers or reinforcers you can examine them and make determinations regarding whether you wish to continue working for these rewards.

> The greatest happiness you can have is knowing that you do not necessarily require happiness.
> —W. Saroyan

Owen Thinker, a rising young professor in the sociology department of Excelsior College, presented a scientific paper, "Social Action and Ecological Reform," that became the manifesto of the Excelsior Conservation Society. Owen Thinker was advised by the college president that academic freedom was a cornerstone of Excelsior College and that because Owen had tenure there was no way he could be stopped from writing or presenting papers. Thinker was reminded that it was his paper that inspired the citizens' group to seek an injunction to stop the offshore drilling by Beachslic Oil Company. The president admonished Owen to consider the consequences. Jeremiah Beachslic was a trustee of Excelsior College and Beachslic

*The president admonished Owen to consider
the consequences.*

Oil had donated the model refinery to the engineering
department. Thinker was also reminded that he was the
logical choice for Dean of Social Science, but that unless
he changed his ways the appointment would go to Professor D. Kaye, who never got involved in contemporary
social issues.

Owen Thinker had always appreciated money and had
looked forward to further promotions and raises. He
stopped and examined his present situation. What would
he do with more money? His life would be essentially the
same. He decided that more money, administrative status,
and Beachslic's approval would not be fulfillment and that
he was in reality already wealthy.

> The gods are those who either have money or
> do not want it.
>
> —L. BUTLER

PETER PRESCRIPTION 11
The Peter Prolongation: *Identify the rewards
at the hierarchal levels above you*

Consider carefully the rewards of promotion so that you
do not become a victim of the carrot-on-the-stick caper.
What would your life be like if you obtained these rewards? Would they be a reinforcement to strive for further gains? Would they bring lasting satisfaction and
peace of mind? Relate the Peter Prolongation to the dis-
coveries you made when applying the Peter Profile. The
Peter Prolongation should help you determine when to
quit escalating at a time and place that will bring lasting
joy and satisfaction.

> 'Tis one thing to be tempted,
> Another thing to fall.
> —W. Shakespeare

PETER PRESCRIPTION 12
The Peter Pry: *Disengage yourself from
influences that are not relevant*

Some individuals are merely a reflection of the social
norms of their community and never understand why they
feel vaguely dissatisfied or suffer from identity problems.

> Let us not say to ourselves that the best truth
> always lies in moderation, in the decent aver-
> age. This would perhaps be so if the majority
> of men did not think on a much lower plane
> than is needful.   —M. Maeterlinck

Tim Iddly was a conformist who tried to avoid conflict
by agreeing with nearly everyone. He purchased only

standard-brand products and attended motion pictures only after he read the reviews. He agreed with his boss, Ty Kune, and laughed heartily each time Ty told one of his oft-repeated jokes. Tim was influenced by endorsements of products by entertainment personalities. He did not stop to consider that the entertainers' own lives were so chaotic that a lack of rational judgment was indicated. Tim Iddly let society shape his behavior and now is in no shape to cope with society.

> He who trims himself to suit everybody will soon whittle himself away.
>
> —R. HULL

Mass production, mass advertising, mass consumerism, and mass faddism have dictated a general leveling of taste and a retreat from individualism. The effect of the advancing depersonalized, mechanistic society must be recognized and analyzed by each of us so that we can be self-directed in those aspects of our lives where individuality is still possible.

> Fate often puts all the materials of happiness into a man's hands just to see how miserable he can make himself with them.
>
> —D. MARQUIS

PETER PRESCRIPTION 13
The Peter Polka: *Sidestep toward success*

Most institutions do not intentionally permit an individual to rise above his first level of incompetence, but history shows that most men who became great leaders had been incompetent followers. As children they had trouble with school authorities and persistently broke the rules and in their early careers were dismissed for insubordination. Under normal hierarchal conditions these men would not reach a leadership position, but in times of war or great social strife the normal promotion system is disrupted and the poor follower is promoted to become a great leader. In desperation a political party nominates a dark-horse candidate. In the heat of battle a man of real leadership takes command. What happens in these situations is that the promotee actually skips or bypasses his level of incompetence to arrive at his level of competence.

Some of our greatest writers failed their language courses in college. They had difficulty getting jobs as journalists, but later, when their creative works were published, their genius was recognized.

> Remember, no one can make you feel inferior
> without your consent.
> —E. ROOSEVELT

Kent Wright was blocked from further promotion because he had difficulty with written detail work. In an emergency situation during a flu epidemic he was called on to handle some pressing business. As acting manager he proved his superior decision-making ability. Consequently he received a permanent managerial position and now willingly assigns all written detail work to his underlings.

> There is something that is much more scarce,
> something finer far, something rarer than ability. It is the ability to recognize ability.
> —E. HUBBARD

Art Pastel was a talented painter but his ambition was to teach art to young children. Unfortunately he was unable to obtain a degree and teaching certificate because he could not pass the mathematics requirement for a degree from Excelsior College. Art transferred to Trifler Technical College, where he enrolled in the mathematics course conducted by Professor Greg Arious. Art's timing was perfect. Greg Arious had just completed his ninth marathon of sensitivity training. He had become so involved with the group scene that his classes were essentially feeling, touching, T-group sensitivity sessions. Art became the most sensitive, open, up-front, uninhibited, actualized student in the class. He passed the course without any mathematics and eventually obtained his degree. He returned to Excelsior College as a graduate student to study for his teaching credentials. Art Pastel had danced a Peter Polka around his area of incompetence and is now happily teaching art. He never gives mathematics a thought.

> Each man must discover his own way.
> —J. SARTRE

Don E. Brook, a shoe salesman at Locount Department Stores, was habitually in disagreement with middle management regarding sales methods. Middle management resented his criticism and so he was barred from promotion. Don joined the Excelsior City Anti-Litter League and was elected president. He conducted a spectacular and effective program for selling the people the idea of a clean city. The board of directors of Locount Stores were so impressed with Don E. Brook's leadership and promotion ability that they invited him to become Vice President of Marketing. Don re-entered the hierarchy at his highest level of competence.

> A man with a new idea is a Crank, until the idea succeeds.
> —M. TWAIN

CHAPTER VII

Know Thy Direction
or
Peep Before You Leap

The heaven of each is but what each desires.
—T. MOORE

THE ultimate purpose of the Peter Prescription is to help you chart a course toward a more rewarding life. Careful consideration of the priorities for your life will help you keep moving forward while you focus on some of the relevant factors that influence your direction in life.

My interest is in the future because I'm going
to spend the rest of my life there.
—C. KETTERING

PETER PRESCRIPTION 14
The Peter Persona: *Develop a concept of
the person you would like to be*

Your self-concept has many facets, including how you perceive your body and physical abilities, how you see yourself in social situations, how you visualize yourself sexually, and how you view your mental abilities. Although all of these are relevant to your direction in life, for purposes of the Peter Persona, focus your attention on your *Humanite self-concept.*

Do you feel that the establishment hierarchy has shaped you into something less than a fulfilled human being? Do you understand the influence the hierarchy has had on your development and how you have been molded by the educational and advertising establishment? If your answers to these questions are in the affirmative, then you are ready to formulate your ideal self-concept.

> For they can conquer who believe they can.
> —Virgil

You live in a world filled with destructive influences that impinge upon you. A self-concept that is consistent with the Humanite vision provides a defense against these influences and contributes to peace of mind and life on your own terms.

Unfortunately, in Western civilization a positive self-concept has too often been equated with aggressiveness, upward mobility, wealth, and material acquisition. These are the very characteristics that when excessively escalated destroy the individual and threaten survival of the human race.

> Golden shackles are far worse than iron ones.
> —M. Gandhi

To strengthen your self-concept, begin by visualizing yourself as a Humanite. Use constructive thought to create an image of yourself as an individual able to determine your own purposes in life. See yourself as living your life free from the escalatory pressures of advertisers, commercial interests, and other manipulators. As your self-concept is translated into action, you become your real self and your constructive thoughts are a beacon to a life in tune with nature.

Our problems are man-made, therefore they can
be solved by man. And man can be as big as
he wants.

—J. F. KENNEDY

Real, constructive mental power lies in the creative
thought that shapes your destiny, and your hour-by-hour
mental conduct produces power for positive change in
life. Develop a train of thought on which to ride. The
nobility of your life as well as your happiness depends
upon the direction in which that train of thought is going.

He who persists in genuineness will increase in
adequacy.

—T. LYNCH

PETER PRESCRIPTION 15
The Peter Proficiency: *Focus your efforts within your area of competence*

At every level of any hierarchy there are opportunities for
fulfillment. You do not have to be president of the mouse-
trap company to build a better mouse trap. As a matter
of fact, as president you would be too busy to give much
thought to designing a better mouse trap. Look to your
experience and concentrate your efforts within your area
of competence.

If you are a university student involved in current
social problems, you should apply your proficiency for
maximum effectiveness. As a science major you can contribute to improvement of environmental quality by using
your scientific skill and the laboratory facilities available
for testing environmental samples. You can then turn your
findings over to mass communicators, conservationists, and
political-action groups. As an English major you can con-

tribute to peace by using your writing skill to describe eloquently the beauty of peace, the horrors of war, and the constructive actions that can be taken to build a peaceful world. As a psychology major you can contribute to social justice through your knowledge of behavior modification and through reinforcing every move made by civic leaders in the direction of social justice. As an engineering, law, education, or medical student you can use your area of competence to contribute to solutions of the problems of your concern.

Escalation might remove you from your area of competence and place you in activities that are counterproductive. This does not mean that you should not participate in political action. It does mean that each student can make an effective contribution through utilization of the skill he is acquiring in the professions, sciences, humanities, or the arts.

> Consider well what your strength is equal to,
> and what exceeds your ability.
>
> —HORACE

Most real improvement in the quality of life is the result of dedicated individuals performing their jobs with art and skill. Much individual discontent, as well as the defects in products and services, is the result of eyes turned upward to higher-level jobs rather than forward to the task at hand.

If the Peter Proficiency were universally applied, it is highly probable that there would be sufficient competence for every position. Society could then value every individual's unique contribution.

> We both exist and know that we exist, and re-
> joice in this existence and this knowledge.
>
> —S. BUTLER

Society could then value every individual's unique contribution.

PETER PRESCRIPTION 16
The Peter Preferment: *Choose the enduring pleasures*

Improvement in the quality of life consists of abiding competence and contentment derived from your life style.

> Enjoy your present pleasures so as not to injure those that are to follow.
>
> —SENECA

Nat Churrell spent much leisure time in the garden of his Northern California home. His patio, swimming pool, and garden provided him with healthful exercise, fresh flowers, fruit, vegetables, and a place of quiet beauty in which to relax and read. He gave all of this up to accept a promotion to the head office in Manhattan. Now with the shorter season for outdoor living and the increased commuting time, Nat Churrell's life provides little contentment.

> Unhappiness is not knowing what we want, and killing ourselves to get it.
>
> —D. HEROLD

When you stop to consider that you may have the enduring pleasures within reach, you will not deny the present for some long-delayed reward.

Performing a job that is not in conflict with your values, sharing with loved ones, and discovering your individuality will produce contentment and lead to a greater sense of personal fulfillment.

> I take him to be the only rich man that lives upon what he has, owes nothing, and is contented.
>
> —S. HOWE

PETER PRESCRIPTION 17
The Peter Potential: *Find a realistic alternate route*

The established hierarchies will not provide satisfaction for everyone. Hierarchal Regression has reached such an advanced stage that many people advocate destruction of the establishment. An alternative with greater potential is to encourage the growth of organizations that will eventually replace the established bureauracy.

> Act well at the moment, and you have performed a good action to all eternity.
>
> —J. LAVATER

Ike O. Noklast, a young lawyer, was concerned about the violation of consumer rights by government, business, industry, and agriculture. No people's lobby existed to hire him to protect them against unsafe automobiles, contaminated foods, or outrageous prices. Although Ike O. Noklast had to work outside the establishment, he was soon joined by supporters and now heads an effective agency protecting consumer rights.

> A heart unspotted is not easily daunted.
> —W. SHAKESPEARE

N. Ventive was employed as a counselor at M. T. Employment Agency. When he observed that his employer made no special effort to place black applicants, he conducted his own survey of employment opportunities in the black community. This resulted in his establishing a successful employment agency for black citizens.

> SATTINGER'S LAW: It works better if you plug it in.

In spite of the entrenched incompetence within the establishment hierarchies, it is still possible to develop effective organizations that are responsive to human needs. With reality as a foundation, some people have left the establishment and formed successful organizations. Others dropped out and failed because they did not assess their potential realistically.

> Real joy comes not from ease or riches or from the praise of men, but from doing something worthwhile.
> —W. GRENFELL

Breaking away from the establishment to open your own competing business, political, or social organization can earn you alienation, distrust, and repression from bureaucrats who stand to lose by your actions. This, along with your competence, is the reality you must assess in determining your potential for success outside of the establishment bureaucracy.

> There are two things to aim at in life: first, to
> get what you want; and, after that, to enjoy
> it. Only the wisest of mankind achieve the
> second.
>
> —L. SMITH

PETER PRESCRIPTION 18
The Peter Predictor: *Foretell your level of competence*

When you are offered a promotion, or at any other decision point in life, do not lose sight of the direction you have chosen. The unwillingness to turn down a challenge has caused many men to change their life goal with each change of job. This results in loss of self, mindless escalation, and the feelings of futility so common in Western man. Greed enables a person to buy things money can buy while losing the things money cannot buy.

> When a man has not a good reason for doing a
> thing, he has one good reason for letting it
> alone.
>
> —SIR W. SCOTT

To achieve your maximum potential, move *forward* toward progressively greater fulfillment. You need never be incompetent through becoming the best human being that your potential, your creative mind, and circumstances will allow.

> There's more credit and satisfaction in being
> a first-rate truck-driver than a tenth-rate execu-
> tive.
>
> —B. C. FORBES

To use escalation to find your maximum potential, you must climb past your level of competence and then, when you realize you are incompetent, move back down to your level of competence. Although this is theoretically possible, in practice it is extremely difficult and meets with uncommon resistance on the part of everyone with an ever-onward-and-upward philosophy.

> To find the optimum position of a worker is like operating a radio receiver. You wish to tune in a station very precisely. You have a meter that indicates signal strength and as you near the optimum point the needle begins to move across the dial. It is not until the needle passes the maximum and starts to fall back that you can be certain that it has reached the maximum.
>
> —J. COLDSTON

PETER PRESCRIPTION 19
The Peter Prognosis: *Anticipate the consequences*

Now that you are aware of the pitfalls and pleasures the establishment has to offer, you will understand that nothing fails like success.

At one time a ship was loaded by men running up a plank with sacks on their backs. But sack carriers, hod carriers, barrow pushers, and the like have been replaced by conveyor belts, forklifts, elevators, and mobile cranes. As rungs are removed from the ladder of human employees you will be nearer Final Placement than you think. Awareness of the inevitable consequences of escalation will help you answer the question, How high is high enough for me?

> By working faithfully eight hours a day, you may eventually get to be a boss and work twelve hours a day.
>
> —R. FROST

118   *The Peter Prescription*

PETER PRESCRIPTION 20
The Peter Possibility: *Try another occupation*

The rate of men leaving establishment jobs to find contentment in new occupations is accelerating. The medical doctor who recently decided to quit his practice and become a writer was not chasing after more money. Like many men today he was bored and wanted to try another occupation.

Men with imagination or a strong creative urge tend to get bored in routine jobs. Change of occupation for the individual with a spirit of adventure is healthy and desirable.

> Since I left university I have spent ten years as a doctor, two years as a merchant seaman, seven years as a businessman, eight as a journalist and fifteen as a novelist.
>
> —J. WILSON

PETER PRESCRIPTION 21
The Peter Pathway: *Let conscience be your guide*

Much mental torment is created through employment that is in conflict with your basic values.

Hiam Atteez enjoyed his work as photographer for the Irvin Blight Advertising Agency. Some of his best pictures were natural landscapes used in the advertisements for Hawk Cigarettes. After the release of the Surgeon General's Report linking cigarette smoking with lung cancer, circulatory disease, and emphysema, Hiam became concerned that his work was contributing to the sale of disease-producing cigarettes. Atteez was now ill at ease.

Hiam submitted a folio of his best scenes of natural

beauty to a conservation group, Friends of the Land, who published the pictures along with Hiam's own descriptive passages. No longer with Irvin Blight, Hiam is now a professional photographer for Friends of the Land. His pictures and writing have awakened thousands to the beauty of their environment and to the need to preserve it. Hiam Atteez now regularly experiences the joy of accomplishment and inner peace.

> Labour to keep alive in your breast that little spark of celestial fire, conscience.
>
> —G. WASHINGTON

CHAPTER VIII

Know Thy Defenses
or
Good Neighbors
Make Good Fences

Do not take life too seriously; you will never
get out of it alive.

—E. HUBBARD

THE most effective defense of your individual capabilities is achieved through maintaining proper direction and through developing your creativity, confidence, and competence.

PETER PRESCRIPTION 22
The Peter Protectory: *Resist the temptation
of escalation for escalation's sake*

In a society based upon upward mobility the offer of a promotion is both flattering and seductive. Even when the individual considers promotion undesirable he usually wants others to be aware that he has received the offer.

They who are all things to their neighbors
cease to be anything to themselves.

—N. DOUGLAS

M. I. Opik was offered a promotion to an administrative post that he considered undesirable. The new position would have tied him to a desk each day and would have required an objectionable change in his present social life. Unfortunately, because M. I. Opik felt that he must prove his worth, he told his wife about the offer. She told her mother and the ladies at her bridge club. M. I. Opik's shortsightedness set in motion a boomerang that returned as profuse congratulations from friends and relatives and pressure from his wife for acceptance of a position that would provide greater social status and an extensive new wardrobe.

> Better a little with contentment than a lot with contention.
>
> —B. Franklin

P. Green, the contented gardener at the Ideal Trivet Company, stayed at his level of competence. He received numerous awards for his flowers and several for his landscaping. His greatest satisfaction was derived through the development of a new variety of gladiolus. It won him first place in international competition, and the sale of the gladiolus corms to professional nurserymen produced a substantial supplementary income. It also provided P. Green with fame and immortality as the flower became known as the Green Gladiolus.

By staying at his level of competence P. Green achieved a sense of fulfillment. He enriched his life through improving and perfecting his performance as a gardener. The horticultural world is now heaping honors upon him.

> Take care of the means and the end will take care of itself.
>
> —M. Gandhi

Although most of the Peter Prescriptions are based upon sound and lasting solutions that help you gain a deeper knowledge of yourself, a better understanding of the hierarchy, and a clearer direction for your life, there are circumstances in which temporary or stopgap measures are called for. The following prescriptions in this chapter are not intended to be permanent solutions. You should feel free to use them whenever your job or level of competence is in jeopardy.

PETER PRESCRIPTION 23
The Peter Playlet: *When threatened with an*
unwanted promotion, pretend you
are already incompetent

The safest and most rewarding Peter Playlet is the performance of side-issue incompetence. For several years I operated a center for the education of handicapped children. This was the fulfillment of a cherished and long-held wish as it provided the opportunity for direct observation and research related to instructional methods. I wanted

Pretend you are already incompetent.

nothing more professionally than to continue this work and complete my research. Because the administration within the university was determined that I should accept a promotion to department chairman, drastic action was called for. When the dean or another official consulted me regarding a question of technical concern, I reached into my desk drawer and obtained a dart which I then threw at a dart board hanging on my office wall. After writing down the number pierced by the dart and using the number repeatedly in an elaborate formula, which I wrote out very rapidly, I then gave a rational or scientific answer to my bewildered questioners. Of course, the ritual of the crazy formula had nothing to do with the answer. This Peter Playlet interfered in no way with my competence, but it did arouse sufficient suspicion to discourage my superiors from promoting me. Through variations on this theme I was able to protect my competence until my research was completed.

During a staff meeting in which my colleagues were trying to persuade me to become department chairman, I walked over to the window and attempted to light a cigarette by concentrating the sun's rays with a large magnifying glass. After a brief silence the meeting resumed with the next item on the agenda. Another Peter Playlet that proved effective was my insistence on proper ceremony in signing contracts and doctoral dissertations. My use of a quill pen, signet, and sealing wax added to the color of the ritual.

The Peter Playlets were a challenge to my creativity, prevented boredom, and satisfied my interest in the dramatic.

> When you tell a dean a joke you have to tell
> him it's a joke or he won't laugh.
> —R. CLOPTON

The ideal Peter Playet is one that (1) does not interfere with the regular competent execution of your job, (2) is a diversionary tactic which focuses the attention of others on irrelevant, unorthodox behavior, and (3) provides you with opportunities for creativity and amusement. Peter Playlets that satisfy these three criteria and that are used with discretion are almost always successful. If you use this prescription excessively you may gain a reputation as a clown and the Playlets will then become ineffective for their intended purpose.

> The perception of the comic is a tie with other men.
>
> —R. W. Emerson

PETER PRESCRIPTION 24
The Peter Parry: *Do not take "the men upstairs" seriously*

Before the publication of *The Peter Principle* I occasionally used a Peter Parry to keep senior officials slightly off-balance. By creating within them a gnawing suspicion that I might not be taking them seriously, I established a situation in which they had sober reservations about having me join them.

The director of the university's doctoral program wrote and distributed an esoteric paper composed of high-level abstractions relating to the philosophy of graduate studies. I responded by sending him a memo congratulating him on the quality of his English prose and for presenting the first understandable analysis of the campus parking problem.

> Humor is an affirmation of dignity, a declaration of man's superiority to all that befalls him.
>
> —R. Gary

Another simple Peter Parry was the innovative use of rubber stamps. Forms that had been completed in the Dean's office were returned with words such as UNTIDY, CENSORED, or CLASSIFIED stamped across them. Standard stamps that are readily available include DO NOT FOLD, APPROVED, RETURNED FOR FILING, and SPECIAL HANDLING. If these are used with imagination they can have the appropriate effect. The more daring can have stamps made to order and thus reap the additional pleasure of seeing his original compositions in print.

> Good taste and humor are a contradiction in terms, like a chaste whore.
>
> —M. MUGGERIDGE

The most successful Peter Parry occurred as an outcome of the publication of the book *The Peter Principle*. Following its success I have received not one offer of a promotion! It appears that administrators have a strong aversion to having within their ranks someone who regards them as suitable subjects for satire.

> THE LAW OF THE PERVERSITY OF NATURE: You cannot successfully determine beforehand which side of the bread to butter.

PETER PRESCRIPTION 25
The Peter Palaver: *Use words to mystify rather than clarify*

The simple declarative sentence is still the greatest tool of written communication ever invented by man. The ability to communicate effectively with your coworkers is an important part of the competence of many jobs. The communication of objectives in precise terms is an essential of competent leadership and is indispensable in any enterprise requiring group participation.

*When someone tries to involve you in something
outside your area of competence.*

When someone tries to involve you in something outside of your area of competence, the ability to reply in
a manner that is essentially noncommunicative is frequently your best defense. Within most hierarchies a
direct refusal is considered to be insubordination. Within
our complex government-industrial hierarchies the competent employee is constantly harassed by inspectors and
investigators of all levels of competence and incompetence. If you are competent in your work and communicate effectively with these officials, the novelty of the
situation so fascinates them that you will spend all your
time writing reports and being interviewed, and you will
no longer be competent in getting your job done. The
only effective defense is the Peter Palaver, a system of
noncommunication.

Before proceeding with the exploration of how to operate the Peter Palaver, please be certain that you under-

stand these two important points: (1) In terms of your on-the-job performance, inability to communicate is incompetence; (2) in terms of defending your job from outside interference, the ability to avoid communication is competence.

> There is great ability in knowing how to conceal ability.
>
> —F. LA ROCHEFOUCAULD

In order for the university to retain the financial support of various state and federal agencies, a great number of official government reports and applications have to be completed. The following samples will illustrate the use of the Peter Palaver in completing these forms:

Question: What method is employed in selection of fellowship students?

Answer: A nonjudgmental on-going reassessment of ego differentiation facilitates role adjustment to the interrelation of consensus work and social integration combining self-determination with an authoritative structured environment.

Question: What is the philosophical basis of the program and how does it relate to teacher certification and the implications of social foundations and the culturally disadvantaged, mentally retarded, gifted, and color-blind child?

Answer: The social involvement objectives are realized by combining a child-centered approach with an accelerated developmental curriculum as an interface with the motivation of interdependent activity of professional effectiveness, utilization, and creative instructional evaluation of accountability. The individual perceptual maturation process and instructional guidance resources enable students to employ environmental orientation in sequential social adjustment to culture.

These are examples of educational officialese, but the technique is the same for any profession. Officialese is a form of bureaucratic writing in which you can understand only the words but none of the sentences. There are two kinds of officialese: one is hard to understand and the other is easy to misunderstand.

> It is necessary to define national interests explicitly. We define national interests as *internally generated and outward flowing forces from within any country which bind that country in some structured way to another country.* National interests are in part physical—hence readily susceptible of quantitative evaluation (numbers of expatriate American citizens; dollars of overseas business investments; volume of foreign trade); in part psycho-social and/or historo-cultural—hence qualitative, intuitive and largely incapable of meaningful quantitative definition; in part entirely abstract (strategic significance of one country to another; the political stance of one country vis-à-vis a third country of mutual significance).
> —J. Brayton Redecker
> Bureau of Inter-American Affairs
> Department of State

At first glance the Peter Palaver may appear difficult but anyone can master it in a few minutes. The simplest and most effective method for beginners is to construct a *Jargon Phrase Indicator.* Let us examine how I developed my educational Jargon Phrase Indicator. First, I collected some words which occurred with great regularity in educational journals, lectures, and documents. I then arranged

them in three lists. The third list consisted of the words
I wished to use as nouns and the first and second lists were
composed of leftover words.

EDUCATIONAL JARGON
PHRASE INDICATOR

1	2	3
perceptual	maturation	concept
professional	guidance	process
environmental	creative	articulation
instructional	relationship	philosophy
homogeneous	motoric	activity
developmental	culture	resource
sequential	orientation	curriculum
individualized	cognitive	approach
exceptional	accelerated	adjustment
socialized	motivation	interface

To use the Indicator I selected at random one word
from the first list, one from the second, and one from the
third. This produced as many phrases as I needed. By
sprinkling a few common Anglo-Saxon words among these
phrases I was able to quickly compose answers to questions, speeches, letters to government agencies, and so
forth.

> The person who uses a lot of big words is not
> trying to inform you; he's trying to impress you.
> —O. MILLER

Follow the same procedure in developing and using a
Jargon Phrase Indicator for any field. The length of the
lists is purely optional. They do not have to be of uni-
form length and you can keep them up to date by adding
words as new jargon becomes popular.

ADMINISTRATION JARGON
PHRASE INDICATOR

1	2	3
interdependent	involvement	objectives
compatible	motivation	utilization
incremental	effectiveness	capacity
optimized	integration	management
optional	transitional	options
quality	digital	contingency
synchronized	organizational	mobility
responsive	monitored	transition
total	integrated	projection
systematized	reciprocal	capability

You can drop phrases such as "quality effectiveness utilization" or "interdependent motivation capacity" into any report so that you will appear to be a knowledgeable authority and at the same time will not be bothered by further questions. If someone persists, continue with your jargon phrases until your questioner retreats in complete confusion.

> The true use of speech is not so much to express our wants as to conceal them.
> —O. GOLDSMITH

The Peter Palaver can be used in two forms—the written form, or The Peter Prose; and the spoken form, or The Peter Parlance. In use both are essentially the same, but there is a special application of the Peter Parlance which I call the Peter Patter, where the method of utterance of the words contributes to the noncommunication. To learn Peter Patter, practice mumbling the key words and phrases of your speech while enunciating clearly such phrases as: Mr. Chairman and gentlemen . . . the time has come . . . let me remind you . . . we must demon-

strate unequivocally . . . our terms are simply . . . let
me make this perfectly clear. . . .

After you have mastered these vocal exercises you may
wish to add further interest by employing alliteration in
which you emphasize the first letter and mumble the
ending of the words.

PETER PATTER JARGON
PHRASE INDICATOR

1	2	3
penetration	peak	pertinacity
prompt	percent	pension
proportion	promulgation	percept
propulsion	propagation	proof
protocol	perseverance	prophylactic
potential	prototype	proposition
pragmatic	proclivity	prospect
polyglot	portrayal	prosthesis
polarity	postulation	perfusion
paradigm	potency	permeation

The Peter Patter is not recommended for beginners.
It requires advanced vocal techniques and complete confidence in your ability to say nothing while talking.

> Look wise, say nothing, and grunt: speech was
> given to conceal thought.
> —W. OSLER

If you have achieved competence, confidence, and
peace of mind you have something worthy of your best
defensive efforts. If your competence is threatened, use
these Peter Prescriptions promptly—delay is decay.

> Guidelines for Bureaucrats: When in charge,
> ponder; when in trouble, delegate; when in
> doubt, mumble.
> —J. BOREN

PART THREE

Manage for Competence

Now that I'm almost up the ladder
I should, no doubt, be feeling gladder.
It is quite fine, the view and such,
If just it didn't shake so much.

—RICHARD ARMOUR

CHAPTER IX

The Competence
Objective
or
All's Well That Ends Well

Of two evils, choose neither.
—C. Spurgeon

You are now well on your way to realizing how to save yourself from the influences that destroy your most important qualities. You are becoming more aware of your individuality and of how to avoid being manipulated into conforming ways of life and patterns of consumerism.

Who can say more than this rich praise, that
you alone are you?
—W. Shakespeare

We will now examine ways in which you can improve your management skills, thereby assisting others in avoiding incompetence. Whenever you consciously influence the behavior of another human being, you are a manager —as is a mother directing the activities of her children, a teacher instructing a class, a conservationist promoting ecological awareness, or a concerned individual influencing other citizens to support an action group.

> The genius of a good leader is to leave behind him a situation which common sense, without the grace of genius, can deal with successfully.
> —W. LIPPMANN

Management can be divided into two classifications: (1) authoritative, in which the directive power resides in the individual manager; and (2) participative, in which the directive power is shared by or emanates from a group of people. The individual who makes decisions and issues orders independently is an authoritative manager and the chairman of a democratically constituted organization is a participative manager. Both are involved in conscious influence on the behavior of others but each derives his power to do so from a different source. The authoritative manager has the power to influence the behavior of others because of his official position, physical strength, or financial resources. The participative manager has power to influence the behavior of others because they willingly consent to be influenced.

> Lots of folks confuse bad management with destiny.
> —K. HUBBARD

If anything is to be created, moved, constructed, or reorganized, the men responsible must have a clear picture of the intended result. Today's objectives are tomorrow's realities, therefore management for competence must be management by objectives. Lacking clearly defined objectives with which to direct energy and evaluate progress, any process can be escalated mindlessly. In a war without clearly defined objectives the commitment of men and resources can be escalated with no way of knowing what is being achieved.

In a social-welfare program without clearly defined objectives, more social workers may be hired and more money expended without anyone knowing what is being achieved—except employment of more social workers and expending of more money. Without predetermined objectives, wherever you arrive is only a matter of chance.

> If you don't know where you are going, you
> will end up somewhere else.
>
> —L. PETER

PETER PRESCRIPTION 26
The Peter Prospect: *Identify your objective*

An objective is a description of what things will be like when a goal has been achieved. It is a statement identifying the intended conditions for the conclusion of an activity.

An objective is different from a direction. It is really a destination. To make more money is a direction, not an objective. A man whose ambition is to make more money has a direction but not an objective. Presumably his escalatory behavior will only come to rest when he has acquired all the money in the world.

In a war being fought without an objective, body counts may be used as an indication of direction. Unless the number of persons killed is related to the achievement of an objective, the escalation of killing will cease only when all those persons presumed to be the enemy are dead.

Usually something intervenes to stop the perpetuation of continuous escalation. Death ends the escalation of the financially ambitious individual. The participants in the war tire of the struggle and find a way out.

> Great blunders are often made, like large ropes,
> of a multitude of fibers.
>
> —V. Hugo

The lack of rationally constructed objectives is evident in many of man's enterprises. Unfortunately, he does not need worthwhile objectives to keep him striving. All he needs is direction, even if it is escalation for escalation's sake or self-destructive escalation to oblivion.

> I'm lost but I'm making record time!
> —*A pilot, somewhere
> over the Pacific*

Shutting down the D. Zaster Mining Company's operations in Deeprest Valley created widespread unemployment in Excelsior County. Federal and state funds were obtained and P. Brayne was appointed as director of a special social-service unit to provide help for the victims of the economic depression. P. Brayne established his office and brought in a staff of social workers and psychological consultants. Each applicant for assistance was interviewed and a case study was initiated. In cases where personal idiosyncrasies were revealed, psychological consultation was provided. Those applicants who were punctual for appointments with their social worker and who were co-operative in the form-filling, testing, interviewing, case-study procedures received financial assistance first. The more dependent they became the greater were the benefits they obtained. The more problems a client presented, the more the social worker felt needed. It was not long before a group of reasonably self-respecting, mature, independent citizens had learned to become multi-problem social-welfare cases. P. Brayne wrote glowing reports describing the variety of services he was providing to meet the complex social, emotional, family-counseling, child-guidance, health, and financial needs of the residents of

Deeprest Valley in Excelsior County. In reality, the direction he had established resulted in the citizens of Excelsior County becoming skilled consumers of social welfare.

> Professional charity—the milk of human blindness. —J. MASEFIELD

One welfare recipient, Owen Mann, was able to obtain employment. His social worker, May Cling, was disappointed and felt rejected by Mann. Her report stated that Mann was not ready for such independent action because he had not completed the series of therapeutic counseling sessions she had arranged.

P. Brayne's program had direction. It provided services and escalated them as rapidly as funds would allow. It lacked objectives. It did not specify the outcomes of the program. It did not describe the kinds of activities to be engaged in by the former employees of D. Zaster Mining nor did it provide any encouragement for those individuals who became occupied by self-help, retraining, or other constructive behavior. P. Brayne was an Unwitting Incompetent.

> A failure is a man who has blundered, but is not able to cash in on the experience.
> —E. HUBBARD

In using the Peter Prospect you must visualize what things will be like if the objective is achieved. You must identify the essential features of the product, describe the performance standards of graduates of the course, or specify what the Deeprest Valley citizens of Excelsior County will be doing. Only when you have a picture of the prospect or of the outcome do you have an objective.

> Many are stubborn in pursuit of the path they have chosen, few in pursuit of the goal.
> —F. NIETZCHE

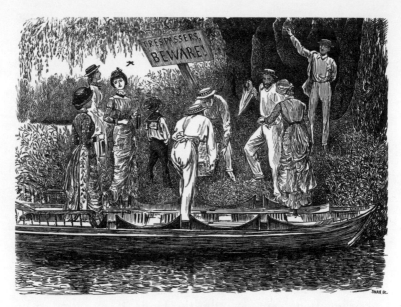

*You must visualize what things will be like
if the objective is obtained.*

PETER PRESCRIPTION 27
The Peter Proposal: *Establish criteria
of successful accomplishment*

The purpose of an objective is to give everyone a means
to decide what has to be done, so that it can be done without constant instruction and direction. Plans and specifications for a building are symbolic representations of its
successful completion. They can be used during construction to establish how much has been achieved and what
has yet to be done to complete the project.

Lacking an adequate objective, a typical management
response is to increase input—hire more people, upgrade
qualifications, urge employees to work harder.

Lacking an objective that defines what the process must
do, individuals may increase input and become busily en-

gaged in useless motions producing enormous activity to accomplish nothing.

> That carpenter is not the Best
> Who makes more chips than all the Rest.
> —A. GUITERMAN

M. Patient, foreman of the Wheel Truing and Bearing Broaching Shop at the D. Rail Train Company, received complaints that his department's work was not standing up on cross-continental hauls. M. Patient, deeply distressed by this information, went to his men and screamed, "Be more careful!" The men, in trying to satisfy their foreman, slowed down their machines and took greater care. The bearings were still returned after short usage. M. Patient, enraged because his men had disappointed him, became angrier in his recriminations. The men slowed down and checked the tolerances more carefully. Unfortunately, M. Patient never established what the problem was nor what constituted a solution. His superiors wanted the bearings to stand up under longer wear. His men assumed he wanted closer tolerances. His shouting and raging did not help establish the fact that the bearing metal was defective.

> Jumping to conclusions seldom leads to happy landings.
> —S. SIPORIN

PETER PRESCRIPTION 28
The Peter Panel: *Involve the personnel in establishment of objectives*

If objectives are to be of maximum value they must be thoroughly understood and accepted. When those responsible for the achievement of an objective participate in the setting of the objective, understanding and acceptance result.

> If his understanding fails, have patience with him.
>
> —SOLOMON

Al Paca, president of Fancy Fleecy Woolen Mills, was worried about the serious competition of Excelsior Synthetics. He told his division supervisors that they must meet this competition or Fancy Fleecy would be headed for bankruptcy. Some weeks later they had their answers. Frank A. Praisal of the weaving department announced, "My department is ready to speed up production by twenty-five percent if the spinning department can provide the yarn." The spinning department manager, Will Spindall, replied, "My department is now ready to produce a better-quality yarn. We will start immediately producing twenty-five percent less than before, but our quality will be superior."

> Here is another bead on the string of confusion.
>
> —W. WOODWARD

PETER PRESCRIPTION 29
The Peter Policy: *Make group goals compatible with individual goals*

An effective manager establishes objectives that help individuals reach their personal goals. Many successful applications of this prescription have occurred in businesses using profit sharing. The employees have similar objectives to management as they both share in the rewards of success.

In recent years there have been some notable violations of this prescription. Some leaders in civil rights and women's liberation at first seemed to have goals that were the same as the goals of the majority of individuals within the group. Later it appeared the leaders were primarily motivated toward personal power and self-aggrandizement. Others with the same needs for personal publicity then arose within the group so that in-fighting flourished among the various faction leaders.

> Those who make peaceful revolution impossible
> will make violent revolution inevitable.
> —J. F. KENNEDY

PETER PRESCRIPTION 30
The Peter Position: *State the objective in terms of the need it serves rather than the form it takes*

Needs are universal and enduring where products and methods become obsolete. The horse and buggy have disappeared, the passenger train is seldom used, ocean liners serve primarily for luxury cruises. These products and methods have decreased while at the same time the need for transportation has grown.

Your objective should not be to build the best movie camera by the year 1985. It should be to build the best live-action recorder. By 1985 movie cameras will probably be replaced by low-cost video recorders.

> It often occurs to me to envy the future for
> what it will know about the past.
> —B. BERENSON

Excelsior Bay was a retirement community on the southern coast a few miles from Excelsior City. Two boating enthusiasts who had experienced financial success in the North set up boat-building companies on opposite sides of the bay. Each wanted a healthier, more enjoyable life centered around his interest in boating.

D. Zion, president of the D. Zion Boat Company on the north side of Excelsior Bay, hired a top naval architect to design the ultimate in the fastest, fanciest motorboats, the sleekest sloops, and the classiest catamarans. He built some fine models that were bought by a few wealthy sportsmen, but in general his business did not do well and his fortune dwindled. Unfortunately, D. Zion went broke and his fine boat inventory was sold under the auctioneer's hammer. D. Zion thought only of the product and not of the need.

> Doubt is not a pleasant mental state, but certainty is a ridiculous one.
>
> —F. VOLTAIRE

Will B. Reddy, on the south side of Excelsior Bay, visualized what a good boat for a retired man with limited boat experience would be like. He drew sketches and showed them to the local residents. Finally he came up with a design that would fill the need. Will B. Reddy decided to concentrate his efforts on producing wide-beamed, rugged, low-performance houseboats. Safe and roomy, they were intended for three things: fishing, comfortable living, and exploring the inland waterways. The hulls were made of extra-rugged Fiberglas and the inboard-outboard engines were easily removed for maintenance and repairs. Will B. Reddy built a boathouse and rented self-help maintenance equipment so that the owners could berth their houseboats and make their own repairs. A mechanic-adviser was available to help any of the owners. Later Will provided a social center, bar, and restaurant. The Excelsior Bay community rapidly converted to boating life and Will's Boathouse became the community center. Will found fulfillment and real happiness through building boats that were in regular use. He rejected several offers from business organizations that tried to buy him out. The competence objective forestalled undesirable escalation and Will B. Reddy continued to be a respected and valued member of the Excelsior Bay community.

> Assuredly nobody will care for him who cares for nobody.
>
> —T. JEFFERSON

PETER PRESCRIPTION 31
The Peter Practicality: *Make the objective one that can be achieved*

Setting an objective that is *possible* to achieve is difficult because so many people are willing to tell you what they think is *reasonable*. Do not confuse "possible" with "reasonable." If you are fifteen years old, skinny, and weak and want to become a professional acrobat, it may not be reasonable but it is possible if you are willing to make the necessary sacrifices. If, on the other hand, you are in the same condition but are fifty-three years old instead of fifteen, your goal is not reasonable and most probably not possible. Your timing is off!

Physically handicapped individuals have achieved success in athletics as well as in other fields, but success was achieved over a long period of consistent practice and there was unusual motivation. Substantial achievement in almost every field of human endeavor is the result of possible objectives, adhered to through a long and sometimes arduous developmental period.

The ten-year objective to put a man on the moon was in itself risky but possible, and with consistent effort the workers lived to see the objective achieved.

> Everything should be made as simple as possible, but not simpler.
>
> —A. EINSTEIN

PETER PRESCRIPTION 32
The Peter Point: *Communicate the objective
by word and deed*

The most effective means of communicating an objective
are: (1) State the objective in concrete terms; (2) provide rewards only for those who move toward the objective; and (3) make your actions consistent with the
objective.

> Actions speak louder than words—but not so
> often.
>
> —Farmer's Almanac

Miss Pearly Gates, a sixth-grade teacher at Excelsior
Elementary School, told her students that she wanted
them to be Excelsior City's top class on the National Scholastic Test. She repeated this objective to them once each
week. During the week, however, she praised students
with the most conforming behavior and neatest papers.
Her students excelled in verbatim memorization, conformity, and neatness. On the National Scholastic Test her
class was one of the lowest in the city. This was quite a
shock to her, since she had told the students how much
the National Scholastic Test meant to her.

The only students who obtained high marks were those
who had set their own objectives. Miss Gates's actions
created a class of well-behaved automatons that pleased
her by being polite, for handing in neat papers, and for
memorizing trivia. These modes of behavior were of little
use when the students came to problem solving on the
National Scholastic Test.

Miss Pearly Gates realized that she had not communicated her objective, so during the next term she escalated

her efforts and told the class twice a week about the importance of the National Scholastic Test.

> He flung himself from the room, flung himself upon his horse and rode madly off in all directions.
>
> —S. LEACOCK

PETER PRESCRIPTION 33
The Peter Portion: *Let others join in the process of establishing interim objectives*

Most substantial objectives are achieved through the accomplishment of a sequence of steps or interim objectives. In Excelsior's east end, across the city from Miss Pearly Gates, Miss Rosie Day taught a class consisting of children from cultural and racial minority groups. Miss Day, like Miss Gates, wanted her class to achieve good grades on the National Scholastic Test because she felt that the children from this run-down neighborhood needed a morale boost before moving on to the Excelsior Junior High School. She began by telling her students that in spite of their past record they should all work toward passing the National Scholastic Test. She solicited their ideas about interim goals as a way of measuring progress toward that objective. The children suggested that they practice answering the kinds of questions that would appear on the test and asked her to obtain some of the old tests from former years.

Miss Day obtained tests for the past six years and listed the questions in order of difficulty. The first week was spent in reviewing the material for her first test composed of the easiest questions. When the test was completed, the students were delighted that they had done so well and began to believe they would be able to pass the final test. Each week they studied for the next of Miss Day's interim tests and by the end of the year were well prepared and confident.

Later, when Miss Rosie Day and Miss Pearly Gates met, Miss Gates said, "Well, of course all your students passed the test. They didn't do anything else but practice for it." Rosie Day was not offended because she knew what her objective had been. Her students had taken their part in developing the interim objectives, and she had taught them to study with a particular goal in mind. They had learned how to learn.

> Reformers are those who educate people to appreciate what they need.
>
> —E. HUBBARD

PETER PRESCRIPTION 34
The Peter Precision: *State objectives in specific, observable, or measurable terms*

It is desirable to have objectives that are observable or measurable so that everyone can recognize when the objectives have been achieved. An objective describing a specific observable outcome has much greater effectiveness than one that is stated in general terms. An objective stating that it is the aim of the *Excelsior Daily Log* to improve its public image does not describe anything that is directly observable. Instead, this objective could be stated as a number of specifics, such as: (1) Within one year, the exterior of the office and plant of the *Excelsior Daily Log* will be painted; (2) grounds will be landscaped with lawn and shade trees; and (3) all street newsstands will be replaced with modern attractive fixtures.

Each general objective—improving environmental quality, beautifying the city, or increasing international understanding—can be stated as a series of specific objectives to facilitate its achievement. The Peter Prescriptions are examples of specific objectives. The general Peter Prescription objective is that you move forward to a better life and avoid escalation to incompetence. This is accomplished through achieving these specific interim Peter Prescriptions.

> It is not enough to know about virtue, then, but we must endeavour to possess it, and to use it, or to take any other steps that may make us good.
>
> —ARISTOTLE

PETER PRESCRIPTION 35
The Peter Peace: *Be satisfied to stop*

In a society based upon perpetual escalation it may at first be difficult to pause and be peaceful. In a world where quantity, wealth, power, and size are valued over quality and self-fulfillment, there is a tendency to mistake escalation for satisfaction.

It may at first be difficult to pause and be peaceful.

Happiness and a state of contentment can only occur in the present. Escalation is an obstacle to contentment. You cannot be happy with what you might obtain in the future—not until that future becomes the present. When you reach that future, will you be content or will you postpone contentment for some other future? When will you enjoy the present? Can you pause and enjoy the happiness that should be yours now? Are you willing to begin to make the present immediately enjoyable by improving your appreciation of the here and now?

> Say wisely, have a care o' th' main chance,
> And look before you ere you leap;
> For as you sow, ye are like to reap.
> —S. Butler

Our obsession with growth has made the world a precarious place in which to live. We have depleted our natural resources, overpopulated, overpolluted, and are rapidly approaching a point where survival is critical. As a survival objective each of us must be willing to stop escalating and start establishing quality objectives rather than quantity objectives. This is the most important of all objectives, because it is the only one that will stand the test of time.

> The quality of American life must keep pace with the quantity of American goods.
> —J. F. Kennedy

CHAPTER X

The Rational Process
or
Think About What
You Think About

It requires a very unusual mind to make an
analysis of the obvious.
                              —A. N. WHITEHEAD

THE rational process separates man from lower forms
of life and gives him the means to avoid his eventual self-
extinction. The rational process is not to be confused with
intelligence. Rather, it is a means of using intelligence.
Frequently intelligence is misused because man confuses
what he would like to believe with what is.

Half our mistakes in life arise from feeling
where we ought to think, and thinking where
we ought to feel.
                              —J. COLLINS

The rational process is taught in schools and universities, yet is seldom put into practice outside of the class-
room. Many well-educated individuals still close their eyes
to events going on around them and act on faith. Most
schools of business administration and management text-

books have complex, formalized procedures for problem solving and decision making—procedures that are hard to follow under the stress of day-to-day life when immediate responses are required.

> The advice of their elders to young men is very apt to be as unreal as a list of the hundred best books.
>
> —O. W. HOLMES, JR.

If you are walking across the street and are approached by a rapidly moving automobile, it is unimportant whether you jump forwards or backwards. The important thing is to get out of the way. Many situations are like this in that a response has to be made immediately.

> When you have to make a choice and don't make it, that is in itself a choice.
>
> —W. JAMES

You can learn to make rational decisions by studying and applying the rational process so that later you will respond rationally under stress. An experienced driver rounds a curve on a mountain road and is confronted with a stalled vehicle obstructing both lanes of traffic. He responds immediately by turning onto the gravel shoulder, and after sliding and swerving in the loose gravel he finally brings his car under control back onto the road. He knows that he has had a close call. He stops his car to rest and recover from the shock, and his mind goes back over the preceding events. He is astounded at the speed at which he made a series of correct decisions in rapid succession.

An inexperienced driver confronted with the same situation panics and rolls his car, and his body is recovered from the wreckage at the bottom of the cliff.

Why the difference? The experienced driver has made many rational decisions while driving under less demanding conditions and is now able to make them as automatic responses in an emergency.

> A great part of courage is the courage of having done the thing before.
>
> —R. W. EMERSON

PETER PRESCRIPTION 36
The Peter Process: *Use rational decision-making procedures*

The rational process requires that you ask yourself *three rational questions,* and that your actions be in agreement with your answers. Everything else involves subtechniques that are helpful and increase efficiency, but if you

A great part of courage is the courage of having done the thing before.

do no more than remember the three questions, you will be able to move toward real solutions.

Three Rational Questions
1. Where am I?
2. Where do I want to be?
3. How do I know I am getting there?

Every man has a sane spot somewhere.
—R. L. STEVENSON

1. Where Am I?

Decision making consists of determining to do something or to do nothing. Deciding to go back to college, to get married, to get a divorce, to change jobs, to go into business, to retire, or to make a policy decision in business should be based upon a realistic assessment of the here and now.

You cannot start from somewhere else. You must begin from where you are. Realistic evaluation of where you are tells you whether you need to make a change and it gives you the basis for determining later if progress has been made.

Apart from blunt truth, our lives sink decadently amid the perfume of hints and suggestions.
—A. N. WHITEHEAD

2. Where Do I Want To Be?

When you have determined where you are, the next logical step is to identify your objective, or where you want to be. If you decide that a change is desirable, what do you intend it to be like after the change is accomplished? If you decide that a problem is to be solved, what are the specifications that the solution must meet?

After you have described your ideal objective you should then study the expenditure of time, money, and effort required to achieve your objective, and alternate routes and methods should be examined so that you can assess the reality of your objective. You may discover that your objective is practical as is or you may decide to modify it in keeping with your resources.

> It is more important to do the right thing than to do things right.
>
> —P. DRUCKER

3. How Do I Know I Am Getting There?

If you wish to make an automobile trip from New York to Los Angeles in five days, you may schedule your first stop in Dayton, Ohio. If you decide on four days, you may have to aim for St. Louis. If you don't make Dayton on your first night, then you will either have to increase your speed or your on-the-road time or extend your overall time. Checking where you are at the end of the first day gives you a measure of progress and lets you know if you are approaching your intended destination.

Many institutions, companies, and individuals escalate without evaluating feedback. When sales are falling, companies add salesmen instead of evaluating their product line. If the customer returns are increasing, they add inspectors instead of investigating the manufacturing processes. Salesmen do not create needs, they only take advantage of them. Inspectors do not improve quality, they only find defects.

> Where there is the necessary technical skill to move mountains, there is no need for the faith that moves mountains.
>
> —E. HOFFER

By plotting your course in advance, both as to milestones and to timing, you can establish progress reports along the way that show deviations from your course. From these reports you can forecast future trends. If you check only your position en route and see that you have moved from your starting point toward your goal, you still have enough of the elements of a rational system to solve most of your problems.

The three questions focus your attention on the starting point, the ending point, and the intermediate measurements. Unless you are one of those people who simply cannot make a decision, the questions automatically elicit decision making.

> There is no more miserable human being than
> one in whom nothing is habitual but indecision.
> —W. JAMES

Consider alternative-action solutions from all possible sources: your imagination, your dreams, suggestions from others, past experience, and technical information. Next, establish a hierarchy of alternatives, weighing the various factors, such as risk, probability of success, practicality, timing, and so forth. Put the Number 1 choice into effect. As long as your chosen action moves you closer toward your target, you need not reconsider your decision. Once the action fails to show progress, it must be re-examined and abandoned if necessary. Do not pursue an ineffective course of activity; there is no stigma attached to recognizing a bad decision in time to install a better one.

> The only man who can change his mind is a
> man that's got one.   —E. WESTCOTT

Once upon a time the United States of Acirema was engaged in an undeclared war in the Far Eastern country of Teiv Man. The war was not going well, so the wise old President, L. B. Jackson, called in his field commander for a briefing. The President looked the military man in the eye and said, "General Wastemoreland, what is our objective in Teiv Man?"

The general stretched to his full height and replied, "To subjugate and pacify the hostile elements."

"And what will that take?" asked L. B. Jackson, looking down at the general from his raised podium.

"Four hundred thousand troops," replied General Wastemoreland, referring to his notes.

"Last year at this time you said you could do the job with two hundred thousand troops," the President reminded him. "I gave you the two hundred thousand troops you asked for; is the hostile element now half pacified?"

"No," replied the general. "As a matter of fact the level of resistance has doubled since the arrival of our troops, making pacification much more difficult."

The President replied, "If two hundred thousand troops doubled the level of resistance, then four hundred thousand troops should quadruple it. General Wastemoreland, this sounds to me like mindless escalation."

Thereupon he fired the general, removed all the troops from Teiv Man, and that country has not been mentioned in the newspapers since.

> They are decided only to be undecided, resolved to be irresolute, adamant for drift, allpowerful for impotence.
>
> —W. Churchill

PETER PRESCRIPTION 37
The Peter Punctuality: *Make your decisions in time for appropriate action*

The correct timing of a decision to act is essential to successful outcomes. The decision to lock the barn door before you put the horse in is just as untimely as locking the barn door after the horse is gone.

Make your decisions in time for appropriate action.

> I have lived long enough to look carefully the
> second time into things I am most certain of
> the first time.
>
> —J. BILLINGS

Will D. Lae was grossly overweight but was fascinated by the idea of becoming a mountain climber. Determined to master the skill, he was able through hard work and continuous practice to develop his arm muscles so that they would support his obese body. He practiced on local slopes and then decided to try his skill on a mountain worthy of his ambitions. He picked the granite face of El Capitan. Halfway up the sheer rock he looked up and was startled to discover that his rope was fraying and in a second or two would break. He looked down and saw that there was no ledge or bush to break his fall. He made a quick decision—he decided to use a heavier rope.

Will's decision was right, but his timing was off.

> The more decisions that you are forced to make
> alone, the more you are aware of your freedom
> to choose. I hold that we cannot be said to be
> aware of our minds save under responsibility.
>
> —T. WILDER

PETER PRESCRIPTION 38
The Peter Prompt: *Strike a balance between
fear and impatience*

It is emotion rather than intelligence that usually prevents
good action solutions. Two of the major psychological barriers are fear and impatience. People generally fall into
one of two categories: They either can't make up their
minds, or they make them up too quickly.

The individual who cannot make up his mind thinks
he is methodical while others think he is overly cautious
or indecisive. On the other hand, the individual who is
always making snap decisions may think of himself as
dynamic while others call him impetuous. Everyone should
learn to give each decision or problem the amount of time
it requires.

> Kill time and you kill your career.
> —B. C. Forbes

N. D. Cysive and Roman Kandel were rival sporting-
goods manufacturers. Both decided that the market for
ski mobiles was going to show dramatic growth and were
determined to take advantage of this.

N. D. Cysive started a survey of potential factory sites.
He found five possible locations, all of which were close
to sources of material, a good potential labor market, and
the snow country—so that transportation and marketing
costs would be at acceptable levels. N. D. Cysive could
not make a choice because the prospective sites were similar in all major characteristics, and so initiated an extensive study program to determine which of the five was
best. He hired a consulting firm and also initiated an in-
house study. Each came up with a different choice. Two
years of additional research has failed to resolve N. D. Cysive's dilemma.

Roman Kandel, impatient to get into production, went directly to his real-estate broker and asked him to locate a factory. The purchase was made and Roman started into production. Unfortunately the area's source of subcontractors was nonexistent, and Roman had to place orders with machine shops hundreds of miles away. Potential dealers for his equipment failed to travel to his factory to examine the prototypes.

The new market went to entrepreneurs who were neither too hasty nor too cautious. N. D. Cysive and Roman Kandel blamed their problems on their subordinates, who they felt had failed to meet the challenge.

> And of all glad words of prose or rhyme,
> The gladdest are, "Act while there yet is time."
> —F. P. ADAMS

In addition to impatience and fear there are many other emotional obsessions established to satisfy needs unrelated to rational thought.

Ivin B. Fore looks to past history for a solution, perhaps for reassurance and perhaps for a future alibi. He examines every decision and finds a solution from prior success stories. Ivin is the country's leading producer of television programs.

I. M. Topps is ego-directed. Decisions must be based upon deference to his status and his hierarchal position. He never backs down on a decision, and will pump money into any idea he has supported long after it has proven hopeless. Topps was the top supporter for the continuation of the Edsel.

Harmony Forall believes that everyone should work together in a friendly atmosphere. A solution that might upset anyone is unthinkable. It makes no difference what is done, so long as nobody is disturbed. Harmony is a budget planner.

Art Icles is paper-directed. The best solutions are found in hardcover books. Next come articles in glossy trade journals. Paperback books are adequate, and agency-originated reports are just barely acceptable and then only if typewritten in triplicate. Without this documentation it is obvious that nothing can be done. Art is the director of emergency-relief funds.

N. C. Cure is fear-directed. His habitual response to any proposition is either "I'm not going to stick my neck out" or "Don't make waves." Cure is an investigator for the public-health department.

Rip A. Sunder is a congenital escalator. Whatever has been done, Rip suggests doing more of the same. When a little doesn't work, he demands a dramatic increase. Rip is a member of the military's famous Think Tank.

> Perhaps man, having remade his environment, will turn around at last and begin to remake himself.
>
> —W. DURANT

PETER PRESCRIPTION 39
The Peter Parsimony: *Make your decisions solution-directed*

The simplest course of action that will do the job is the one to select. In the hierarchy of solution characteristics simplicity must be near the top—it yields so many untold benefits and avoids so many unseen pitfalls.

> Many people fail because they conclude that fundamentals simply do not apply in their case.
>
> —M. L. CICHON

PETER PRESCRIPTION 40
The Peter Partition: *Separate the solution*
from the people problem

Almost every solution has a built-in people problem—a
reason why you cannot do exactly what you would like
to do. First establish your objective and then determine
the adjustments required to make the solution palatable,
or workable. When it is not possible to overcome built-in
prejudices, it is best that they be recognized and provided
for.

> I am free of all prejudice. I hate everyone
> equally.
>
> —W. C. Fields

Happy Landon, the director of a community-action
agency in Excelsior City, decided that the ghetto needed
a minority-run business enterprise. There were fierce rival-
ries among the various minority groups that made it necessary to set up the new enterprises so as to satisfy all
groups. Happy established this as the first priority for his
business consultants. The consultants suggested a clothing-
manufacturing plant centrally located on geographically
neutral ground, and staffed with executives, managers,
supervisors, and workers from all groups, equally distributed in all job categories. The project was inaugurated
with a fanfare of publicity portraying it as a model of
integration-at-work.

From the start the company floundered. The executives
saw things differently insofar as styling and price range
were concerned. The subordinates did not follow instructions, each believing that his power came from the minority group that backed him. The clothes that were produced
did not please anyone, having been created out of agoniz-
ing compromises. In eighteen months the factory closed.

Minority-group co-operation had been dealt a serious blow.

> A prejudice is a vagrant opinion without visible
> means of support.   —A. BIERCE

Happy Landon had learned a lesson and so he tried again. This time he decided that the Number 1 priority was for the business to be successful. He formed a board of minority-group members and told them that he would refuse to embark upon any task that was doomed from the start. If they wished to have minority-run businesses, the directors would have to approve a workable plan and then sell their minority groups on supporting it, even if at times the distribution of power and jobs appeared inequitable. The profits would be shared by all groups and would be utilized in starting new businesses for the other groups.

After many proposals and rejected plans the group finally agreed upon a paper-goods factory located entirely in a black neighborhood and manned predominantly by blacks. The other minorities were urged to support the factory by buying its products. As the factory grew, the community became enthusiastic about the program and supported Happy Landon's new ventures.

> Men have dignity . . . only in so far as they
> share in the attempt to advance the common
> welfare.
>   —A. MEIKLEJOHN

PETER PRESCRIPTION 41
The Peter Promise: *Watch for the decision
no one asks you to make*

The most fleeting of all things is opportunity. It rarely knocks twice and sometimes does not knock at all. Conversely, misfortune seeks your unaware moment. You must be aware both of opportunities and of unsuspected dangers.

> There is a limit at which forbearance ceases
> to be a virtue.
>
> —E. BURKE

In 1948 Remington Rand * bought the UNIVAC corporation from the inventors of the electronic computer, John Mauchly and John Presper Eckert. What competition existed at that time was negligible.

Remington Rand (now Sperry Rand) did not completely discount the potential of the digital-computer market, but UNIVAC was just one division out of many in their large corporation. The Remington Rand management spent most of its efforts trying to fit UNIVAC into the mold of their other divisions. They insisted on similarity of management, of marketing, and of customer servicing. Top management did not perceive that this market was different—it was a new industry in itself.

Remington Rand was so involved in improving the operational details that it allowed the sleeping International Business Machine Corporation to wake up. IBM so thoroughly captured the computer market, starting from zero in 1950, that most people today think that IBM originated and invented digital computers. The profits that Remington Rand lost because of unawareness far exceed the losses sustained by Ford on the Edsel, General Dynamics on the 880 aircraft, or any other textbook case of industrial misdirection.

> If you are hunting rabbits in tiger country,
> you must still keep your eye peeled for tigers,
> but when you are hunting tigers you can ignore the rabbits.
>
> —H. STERN

* Names used in this case are not fictitious.

PETER PRESCRIPTION 42
The Peter Potency: *Have the courage to act*

The rational process clarifies thought, but even the timid can be taught to think clearly. Reason without action is a eunuch. Once you have decided what must be done you must put forth energy to make your objective come true. If you know where you are, and you know where you want to be, nothing should deter you from your journey—not fear or doubt or ridicule. Any start in the proper direction, no matter how small, brings you closer to your goal.

> No great man ever complains of want of opportunity.
>
> —R. W. EMERSON

In any endeavor be sure you define your goal, picture yourself in the environment of your goal, see if you would really like it. There should, however, be no self-deception or wishful thinking about your present location—define it as it is. It is the rational process that gives you the blueprint for moving forward and protects you from the Final Placement Syndrome.

> A tomb now suffices him for whom the whole world was not sufficient.
>
> —*Epitaph for* ALEXANDER THE GREAT

CHAPTER XI

The Gift of Prophecy
or
The Future Lies Ahead

Old men and comets have been reverenced for
the same reason: their long beards and pre-
tenses to foretell events.

—J. SWIFT

THROUGHOUT the ages man has attempted to foretell the
future by utilizing mystical procedures. Although none of
these procedures have increased his ability to predict the
events to come, he still persists in such irrational en-
deavors. Crystal gazing, palmistry, astrology, and card
reading capture the imagination, and when an occasional
prediction is fulfilled, it supports wishful thinking and
belief in mystical powers. While little has been accomplished in reliable prediction through the magical or
mystical processes, great progress has been made in the
scientific prediction of future events.

MALINOWSKI'S LAW: Looking from far above,
from our high places of safety in the developed
civilization, it is easy to see all the crudity
and irrelevance of magic.

All science is concerned with the relationship of cause
and effect. Each scientific discovery increases man's ability

to predict the consequences of his actions and thus his ability to control future events.

> Most of our so-called reasoning consists of finding arguments for going on believing as we already do.
> —J. H. Robinson

A true science must be based upon accurate observation of objective reality. Unfortunately, much that is disguised as social science is based upon subjective opinion, wishful thinking, and unsubstantiated theories.

> The obscure we see eventually, the completely apparent takes longer.
> —E. R. Murrow

In social science, as in physical science, the more accurate the observation, the more predictable the results. Direct observation of human behavior provides the best basis for making accurate personnel predictions.

Each of the following Peter Prescriptions is based upon the scientific method and will help you increase the probability that your decisions will prove to be correct in the future.

> To profit from good advice requires more wisdom than to give it.
> —J. Collins

In most cases people decisions are the most important and are most prone to error. A wrong decision in people selection can sabotage the best organization plans and scientific, technical, or industrial capabilities.

> Things are easier said than done, unless you are a stutterer.
> —R. Lewton

We all wish for complete or utopian security but we must accept that this is only fantasy. We live in a world

of uncertainty where the most difficult puzzle is man himself. This shall always be, because man studying man can
never be completely objective.

> HARVARD LAW: Under the most rigorously con-
> trolled conditions of pressure, temperature,
> volume, humidity, and other variables, the or-
> ganism will do as it damn well pleases.
>
> —A. S. SUSSMAN

PETER PRESCRIPTION 43
The Peter Probability: *The scientific method,
your true gift of prophecy, only shows you
the approximate shape of things to come*

Deciding not to decide is in itself a decision. When we
make a decision to promote or not to promote an employee, to hire or not to hire an applicant, or to transfer
or not to transfer a staff member, we would like to be
able to predict the outcomes of that decision accurately.
The very best we can do is improve the probability that
the decision is the correct one.

> Thoughts are but dreams till their effects be
> tried.
>
> —W. SHAKESPEARE

Upon the resignation of B. Wright, a competent
manager for Excelsior Rope Products, chief executive
C. Clearly recognized that, desirable as it might be, he
could not replace B. Wright with another B. Wright. He
realized that Wright had made a unique contribution
through his creative leadership. C. Clearly understood
that B. Wright's successor should make his own contribution and so appointed A. Newman, who, as well as showing administrative ability, was interested in the problems
of civil rights. In his new position Newman successfully

We live in a world of uncertainty.

involved his department in improving the job opportunities for minority workers in Excelsior City. C. Clearly and the directors at Excelsior Rope were satisfied that Newman had shown the company new ways it could adapt to changing social conditions.

> The well-developed, well-patterned individual human being is, in a strictly scientific sense, the highest phenomenon of which we have any knowledge; and the variety of individual personalities is the world's highest richness.
>
> —J. HUXLEY

Magnus Fogg, general manager of Perfect Pewter Propellers, needed an immediate replacement for D. Seller, who had been made international sales manager. Fogg promoted the Excelsior City sales manager, Slim Pickens, and told him that he had been so pleased with Seller that all he wanted was for Pickens to do exactly as Seller had done. As a result Slim Pickens spent half his time trying to guess what Seller would have done and the other half in repeating Seller's methods in situations where they were inappropriate or had become obsolete.

> Nothing is enough to the man for whom enough
> is too little.
>
> —EPICURUS

PETER PRESCRIPTION 44
The Peter Particular: *Define the job clearly*
before the candidate is selected or promoted

Quite different skills, talents, and aptitudes are needed for a dogcatcher as compared to a baseball catcher, a marketing engineer contrasted to a construction engineer, or a salesman to a sales manager.

Job titles lack precision because, even though the title may be the same, the actual requirements and expectations vary from company to company or agency to agency.

> Definitions would be good things if we did not
> use words to make them.
>
> —J. ROUSSEAU

Sarah Bellam, Dean of Excelsior Stenographic School, decided to promote a teacher to the newly created position of co-ordinator of instruction. The school's two outstanding teachers were Sophie Tutch and Gerda Jobdun. The students enjoyed the freedom of Sophie Tutch's classes, where they discussed issues relevant to their interests. To a large extent she let her classes run themselves. Sophie Tutch did not hold her students to rigid deadlines as Gerda Jobdun did. Miss Jobdun's students learned much more stenography, but when Sarah Bellam polled the students on their favorite teacher, Sophie Tutch won the contest. As co-ordinator of instruction, Sophie continues to be vague and unorganized. Competent in a popularity contest, she was incompetent as an administrator.

> About the only person we ever heard of that wasn't spoiled by being lionized was a Jew named Daniel.
>
> —G. D. Prentice

With the rapid expansion of Mercury Disposable Products it was decided to create a new position, that of Vice President of Marketing. The company president, B. Hasty, insisted that the position be filled at once. He selected Oslo Learner, a hardworking employee from the marketing department. Hasty said, "Whew! Is that a load off my mind." Oslo Learner proceeded to prove that a hard worker is not always a good worker. Hasty's solution to Oslo's mismanagement was to create a new position, Assistant Vice President of Marketing. "It's a critical position!" he announced. "We have got to fill it at once!" And another innocent victim was misguided to his level of incompetence.

> O wad some Pow'r the giftie gie us
> To see oursels as others see us!
>
> —R. Burns

PETER PRESCRIPTION 45
The Peter Proof: *Try before you buy*

When you have identified your objective, it is good practice to try a variety of solutions to find which best meets your requirements.

> The uncreative mind can spot wrong answers, but it takes a creative mind to spot wrong questions.
>
> —A. Jay

To see oursels as others see us!

Stan Doffish, engineer in charge of painting traffic lines on Excelsior City streets, wrote specifications describing the street and highway surfaces and the conditions to which road paint would be subjected. Specifications were sent to suppliers and small quantities of the recommended paints were ordered. Doffish tested these on the streets of Excelsior City. When he ordered a large quantity of the paint that stood up best in the trials, he did so with a high degree of confidence that the paint would be successful in future applications.

> Science is a collection of successful recipes.
> —P. Valéry

In making personnel decisions it is frequently possible to utilize the same general procedure that was successful in selecting paint for Excelsior City streets.

> Very simple ideas lie within the reach only of complex minds.
> —R. de Gourmont

Francis Gaye was Excelsior City's most successful beauty-salon operator. After several prominent women became his patrons he opened a second Mr. Gaye Salon. His assistant, Mr. Plume, managed the second salon so well that soon Mr. Gaye was planning to open salon Number 3. Mr. Gaye and Mr. Plume discussed potential managers. Mr. Marcell was competent but appealed only to the older ladies. Mr. Bouffant had a great chairside manner but he would not change his hair styling to keep up with the times. Mr. Chic was ideal. He was creative, modern, handsome, and personable. Mr. Gaye was ready to offer Mr. Chic the managership immediately, but Mr. Plume suggested a more cautious approach. Plume said, "I am taking my holidays soon, so why don't you sample Mr. Chic's managerial ability while I am away?"

When Mr. Chic was offered the position of acting manager for three weeks, he was thrilled at the opportunity and full of confidence. Plume gave Chic a thorough briefing and then left on his vacation. During the first day as acting manager Mr. Chic phoned Mr. Gaye twelve times regarding routine matters. By the second day Chic was phoning about petty complaints regarding the operators in the salon. By the end of the second week he was monopolizing Mr. Gaye's time with gossip about the relationships and jealousies of his staff, trivial organizational questions, and complaints about his burden of responsibility.

This sample of Chic's behavior formed an adequate basis for deciding that he lacked the emotional stability required for managerial responsibility. He preferred to complain about a problem rather than deal with it.

A three-week sample of Chic's managerial behavior was not enough to explore his full potential for mismanagement but it did reveal his hitherto undisclosed areas of incompetence.

> To the small part of ignorance that we arrange
> and classify we give the name knowledge.
>
> —A. BIERCE

Many situations occur in the normal course of events that provide opportunities to obtain samples of a prospective promotee's relevant behavior, but few take full advantage of these opportunities.

Frequently men have promoted highly competent girlfriends to the positions of incompetent wives. Situations were not arranged to test their prospective mates' conduct as partners in homemaking, budgeting, or stressful marital situations. Many women have promoted competent boyfriends to the roles of incompetent husbands without first testing to see how they would respond in future life situations.

> Said Simple Simon to the pie man,
> "Let me taste your wares."
>
> —S. SIMON

PETER PRESCRIPTION 46
The Peter Pretest: *Apply the hidden test formula*

In contemporary hierarchies a promotion is seldom rescinded. For this reason it is good practice to obtain a secret test of an employee's possible future behavior before promoting him.

> There's only a step from the sublime to the
> ridiculous, but there's no road back from the
> ridiculous to the sublime.
>
> —L. FEUCHTWANGER

Dr. Ben E. Fishel, superintendent of schools for the Excelsior educational district, was faced with the problem of recommending to the board of education a suitable

*To test their prospective mate's conduct as partner
in stressful marital situations.*

candidate for the position of principal of a new elementary school. Two successful teachers had each completed
a graduate degree in administration and were equally
qualified. Ben E. Fishel interviewed each of them sepa-
rately and questioned them about their educational phi-
losophies and attitudes. Miss Grace Lovejoy and Mr. Red
Whitenblu each replied with standard approved answers,
such as, Education reflects the values of society, and
Schools should exemplify the democratic process as presented in the basic documents of the country. They both
stressed their love for children and respect for parents.
Up to this point in each interview there was little to base
a choice upon between the candidates.

Dr. Ben E. Fishel then handed each candidate a sheaf
of notes and letters. He said, "Unfortunately I have been
unable to take any of the new courses in educational
administration. Here are some problem letters that prin-
cipals have sent to me this past week. Could you help me?

Look them over and give me your opinion about each."
He then handed over the first letter.

> Dear Principal,
>
> I am Otto Hood and I own the Excelsior
> Body Shop. Business has been tough recently
> because of unfair competition. My son, Mike
> Hood, says that yesterday he received cor-
> poral punishment from his teacher simply for
> knocking down some boys and girls who did
> not get out of his way in the hall.
>
> I am a taxpayer and I am paying for Mike
> to be taught, not to be punished. I do not
> know why he hits other children. He does it
> a lot, but I give him a sound thrashing every
> time I catch him at it. I give him enough beat-
> ings that you would think he would stop hitting
> people.
>
> I have to beat him but teachers should use
> psychology. I did not go to college so did not
> learn psychology. What is the use of all that
> teacher training if that is all the good psy-
> chology does?
>
> Yours truly,
>
> Otto Hood.

Miss Grace Lovejoy said, "Dr. Fishel, I think I would
phone Mr. Hood and offer to see him. I would express
concern for his business worries, but would focus the
conversation on Mike's problems. I would also tell him
about the counseling and psychological services provided
by the school district in case he wished to use them."

Dr. Fishel then asked Miss Lovejoy why she would not
discuss the question of corporal punishment. She replied,
"I would not bring it up, unless Mr. Hood did. He may
have used this incident as his way of expressing his frus-

tration regarding Mike's behavior. The letter may have been an appeal for help."

Mr. Red Whitenblu said, "That's the problem with parents today—always criticizing teachers. What do they know about education? Hood can't even manage his own kid and yet he has the nerve to find fault with the school for trying to maintain discipline."

Dr. Fishel asked Red Whitenblu what he would do about the letter. Whitenblu replied, "I would write a letter to Mr. Hood quoting the State School Law #402, Section D, Item 6: 'A teacher shall employ the discipline of a judicious parent.' That should put Otto Hood in his place."

Grace Lovejoy responded to each situation presented in the correspondence with understanding and sound educational solutions. Red Whitenblu responded with hostility, a lack of understanding, and with proposals that were counterproductive.

Later Dr. Ben E. Fishel was satisfied that he had obtained a representative sample of Miss Grace Lovejoy's behavior. As principal of West Excelsior Elementary School, she gained affection and respect in the community and was admired by both faculty and pupils.

> When love and skill work together, expect a masterpiece.
>
> —C. READE

Many opportunities exist for application of the Peter Pretest. An employee can be asked to help out at a higher-level job or can be given problems to solve and correspondence to answer. These practices can obtain a representative sample of the behavior required in the new position.

> By a small sample we may judge of the whole piece.   —M. DE CERVANTES

B. Loanee was a competent bookkeeper at National Loan and Truss Company. He never lost track of a penny. Branch manager Bill Folder rewarded Loanee's competence by a promotion to loan counselor. B. Loanee proved that a good accountant does not always make a competent moneylender. He accurately recorded how each company misspent its way to bankruptcy.

The new superintendent of Treadless Tires, Inc., realized the company was in a rut, so he made some changes. One was to promote a very competent accountant, D. Sifer, to a managerial position. D. Sifer was a genius with numbers but a disaster with personnel.

> Success has made failures of many men.
>   —C. ADAMS

PETER PRESCRIPTION 47
The Peter Play: *Simulate the specifics of future reality*

Frequently role play can capture the essence of reality and the individual will behave in ways equivalent to the ways he will behave in future situations.

Group dynamics, sociodrama, and psychodrama have each demonstrated that, given a role to play and no script to follow, most individuals will behave much as they would in a real-life situation. Management development has used this kind of simulation to good effect. It is best employed in a workshop situation where everyone can enter into the spirit of the game. The participants take turns playing the different roles. Each may have a turn as the supervisor dealing with petty, demanding, complaining, and flattering employees, or as the inconsiderate and capricious superior. These simulations reveal with considerable accuracy how each individual would respond in real situations. By reversing roles and playing various parts, the participants have opportunities to improve their performance. The participant may play the part of a manager interacting with an aggressive competitor, a demanding chief executive, a picky difficult customer, and an irresponsible employee, and reveal how he would function in the real situation.

> Don't rely on the label on the bag.
> —T. Fuller

PETER PRESCRIPTION 48
The Peter Petition: *Try a temporary promotion*

A tragic error occurs when a man who is doing a job well is promoted to a position of incompetence. It is almost impossible to unpromote him.

Trial promotions if sensitively handled can be utilized in certain situations. When a position is available, those qualified are invited to petition for a trial period. After careful discussion of the criteria and objectives for the position, an applicant is given a trial period. During this time he is encouraged to discuss his feelings, satisfactions, and frustrations. Near the close of the trial period the potential promotee can frequently make a realistic evaluation that leads to a valid decision regarding whether to continue or return to the former position. This can be successful only in an organization where healthy attitudes toward human values exist. Traditional values regarding upward mobility limit the situations in which the Peter Petition can be utilized effectively.

> Deliberating is not delaying.
> —Ecclesiasticus

PETER PRESCRIPTION 49
The Peter Propagation: *Develop the new promotee*

You can substantially increase the chances of a potential promotee's becoming competent by preparing him for the future.

When a salesman is promoted to sales manager he must acquire a whole new repertoire of skills and attitudes. He must learn to deal with some problems at an abstract or symbolic level when planning sales territories, promotion campaigns, and record systems. As an administrator he must derive his satisfaction from the achievement of others. Many high-powered solo performers have difficulty when they try to make the transition from performing a task to managing others.

The successful and talented engineer with an impressive record of solving technical problems may be impatient and overbearing when promoted to a management position. Competent at dealing with things, he may still need to acquire new competence in the management of personnel.

To help the salesman, technician, engineer, or other professional make the transition to competent management, it is essential to first define the job, its requirements, and the criteria of success, so that the promotee will be able to establish objectives and evaluate results. There is a tendency for the salesman or engineer to think of the promotion as an increase in prestige and salary and an opportunity to be a salesman or engineer with new authority and position. To avoid such misconceptions it is necessary for the promotee to identify the difference between what he did in the past and the duties of a competent manager. As a manager he will no longer derive his satisfaction from his direct contributions to the state of the art of his profession. He will have to derive his satisfaction from the accomplishments of others through motivating, developing, and integrating their activities toward shared objectives.

Discussion of these basic managerial, attitudinal, and behavioral requirements with the potential manager will increase the probability of future success. For some it will result in a decision that management is not for them. Either way, future competence is enhanced.

> Anything that makes the world more humane
> and more rational is progress; that's the only
> measuring stick we can apply to it.
> —W. LIPPMANN

PETER PRESCRIPTION 50
The Peter Perception: *Listen with your third ear*

Interviewing is a favored technique in selecting new members for a hierarchy and for escalating individuals already situated within a hierarchy.

In what I call Hiring Situation U, the applicant is unemployed and is seeking work. He is in effect seeking promotion from the rank of Unemployed to that of Suitably Employed. "Suitably" is a subjective term. You cannot always tell whether the applicant will consider your job offer a promotion. At times you will have to make a quick estimate of the applicant's Desperation Quotient in deciding what to offer him.

In Hiring Situation E the applicant is employed. Here he is seeking a promotion within your organization (an intrahierarchal promotion) or is considering moving from another hierarchy to yours (an interhierarchal promotion).

A competent interviewer correctly applies the criteria

prescribed by the hierarchy and determines who is fit for employment or promotion. The interview can be a valuable contribution to the assessment process. You can size up the applicant and see whether he sounds and looks good to you. Remember that this is your subjective opinion. The interview is not a substitute for the previously discussed techniques nor for investigation of academic or technical qualifications, testimonials, work records, medical reports, etc.

The Play's the Thing

Each interview is, in essence, a small-scale theatrical performance. The applicant tries to act the role of "competent employee." The interviewer is the critic evaluating the performance.

The prudent applicant has studied his part in advance. He knows precisely how this hierarchy defines competence, and on that knowledge bases his portrayal of competent employee. All that the interviewer can decide is whether the applicant can or cannot play the part for the duration of the interview. The question of whether the applicant can continue to portray competent employee for weeks, months, or years is not resolved in the interview, nor is the question of whether he even wants to continue the performance. Let us now examine how the applicant fares with incompetent and competent interviewers.

INCOMPETENT INTERVIEWER The incompetent interviewer does not realize that the applicant is playing a role. He mistakes the mask for the face. Early in the interview he decides that he likes or dislikes the applicant.

There is less to this than meets the eye.
—T. BANKHEAD

He does not realize that the applicant is playing a role.

C. Nile had to select a new inventory manager. He could choose either Strom Gimage or Nick Alodeon. During the interview he noted that Strom bore a striking resemblance to Fred Founder, who had built the company back in the early 30's. Strom Gimage got the job in spite of Nick Alodeon's proven competence and years of experience.

This example shows that it is often appearance, not performance, that counts.

> Things are seldom what they seem,
> Skim milk masquerades as cream.
> —W. GILBERT

The incompetent interviewer judges an applicant by secret preferences based upon physical attributes, religion, race, politics, mannerisms, age, or sex, rather than on the employee's potential.

> Don't rely too much on labels,
> For too often they are fables.
> —C. SPURGEON

B. Upleigh, personnel manager of the Dainty Daisy Deodorant Division of Dr. Dung's Chemical Corporation, interviewed Frank Ness for the position of consumer-relations director. Upleigh was impressed with Frank Ness's candor and honesty.

As director of consumer relations Frank Ness frequently raised a stink. He admitted to a reporter that there should be a ban on spray cans because inhaling the deodorant was harmful. He further admitted that he did not know if Dainty Daisy caused skin problems. He then announced that if Dr. Dung was successful in stopping perspiration, he would not be satisfied until he had suppressed all other bodily functions. Frank Ness was recently reprimanded for telling M. Potent, founder of the M. Potent Sedative Division, that he had perspiration odor. Frank was over-qualified in the honesty area for the job Upleigh gave him.

> Don't hire a chemical engineer to brew you a cup of coffee.
>
> —A. MARGOLESE

Stu Pidd, athletic director for Excelsior City Schools, interviewed B. Ragger for a position as baseball coach. B. Ragger said, "On my last team, I starred in all nine positions, led the team in hitting, fielding, pitching, and stealing. In most games I was the one to make the winning play."

In his new position as coach he spends his time regaling the children with tales of his past glories rather than helping them develop their abilities.

> Men govern nothing with more difficulty than their tongues, and can moderate their desires more than their words.
>
> —B. SPINOZA

COMPETENT INTERVIEWER   The competent interviewer knows that the applicant is playing a role. He tries to peek behind the mask and see the real face. He recognizes that the bright, clean-cut applicant sitting before him may have sobered up, shaved, bathed, and had his clothes cleaned and pressed for this interview.

The competent interviewer withholds judgment and listens carefully. He listens to the content of what the applicant tells him and with the third ear listens to the tone of the applicant's remarks. Is he really secure in the role of competent employee, or is he a pompous braggart trying to conceal his insecurity or incompetence? Is the applicant's nervousness the result of inexperience in the interview situation or is it a symptom of his Desperation Quotient? What are his aspirations and apprehensions? Is this role consistent with his experiences and are there inconsistencies in the interview itself?

> You can see things, and you say, "Why?" but I see things that never were and I say, "Why not?"
>
> —G. B. Shaw

PSYCHOLOGICAL TESTS   Psychological tests as predictors have been so abused, misused, and oversold that space does not permit an adequate explanation of their strengths and limitations. Pioneer advocates of aptitude tests would do away with such subjective procedures as interviews, work records, or recommendations. But tests are now seen as somewhat subjective themselves, reflecting the personalities and prejudices of those who compile them and of the samples of subjects upon which the tests are standardized. Test results should not be a substitute for judgment but they can provide a measure of objectivity that can assist in the decision-making process.

> Aptitude tests show that you will succeed in a business where your father is boss.
>
> —P. Sieler

Predicting human behavior is complex, and the competent manager of human destinies must utilize the Peter Prescriptions that are appropriate to his specific situation. If the manager has reached his level of incompetence, it matters little what techniques he attempts to employ. Results will probably be unsatisfactory, competent applicants will be rejected, some will be promoted to levels of incompetence, and others will be assigned to the wrong positions. Nevertheless, even an incompetent manager will make some correct decisions by chance just as a chimpanzee pounding a typewriter will produce some correctly spelled words.

> The challenge to think systematically about large, ambiguous questions is inherently daunting, and is one that many businessmen—activists by nature—may be reluctant to take up. But if businessmen are to manage events, rather than be managed by them, there is no alternative.
>
> —W. S. RUKEYSER

CHAPTER XII

The Compensation Miracle

or
Why Man Behaves
as Man Behaves

The trouble with our age is all signposts and
no destination.
                                    —L. KRONENBERGER

B EFORE you engage in competence motivation you should
(1) know the objectives you are attempting to achieve,
(2) apply the rational process, and (3) predict the results
of your decisions. It is only after you have applied these
prescriptions that you are justified in utilizing compensation to actually change behavior.

I want to change things. I want to see things
happen. I don't want just to talk about them.
                                    —J. K. GALBRAITH

In earlier times the majority of men had to work to earn
their daily bread. Their compensation for working was
survival. In the case of slaves, work was also required to
avoid the pain of the lash. Social and technological changes

*The trouble with our age is all signposts
and no destination.*

have altered this situation so that it is no longer necessary
to work in order to avoid being whipped or starved. The
contemporary scene requires that more humanistic and
subtle compensation methods be used.

> All the beautiful sentiments in the world
> weigh less than a single lovely action.
> —J. LOWELL

The ultimate goal of compensation is to produce competence. If our objective is to save civilization, our
nation, or our major institutions from Hierarchal Regression, each hierarchy must be staffed by competent
Humanites. We need motivated, competent, responsible
individuals as citizens, employees, administrators, and directors. Before you can perform compensation miracles
competently, you will need to understand how the motivated, responsible, competent Humanite develops.

My mother loved children—she would have
given anything if I had been one. —G. Marx

Children under favorable conditions develop into individuals who possess competence, concern for others, ability
to give and receive affection, and motivation toward worthwhile goals.

Babies are such a nice way to start people.
—D. Herold

From birth through the first few months of life, satisfaction is derived through gratification of physical needs.
When Baby is hungry his dissatisfaction is expressed in
crying, facial expression, bodily tension, and jerky move-
ments of his arms and legs. As the baby is fed, his crying
ceases, his body relaxes, and his cheeks become full, taking on a rosy glow as he breathes more deeply and con-
tentedly.

Physical contact also produces satisfaction during early
infancy. Cuddling, patting, and stroking are originally less
satisfying than food but they gradually increase in importance through pairing with food. Mother holds and cuddles
Baby close to her warm body during feeding. This pairing
of physical contact and feeding increases the satisfaction
that can later be produced simply by holding.

When food and drink are presented by a loving mother
who hugs, kisses, rocks, and pats the baby, these social
contacts become highly satisfying, and Baby has made
his first important step in socialization.

A babe in a house is a wellspring of pleasure.
—M. Tupper

Satisfying emotional responses to food and physical contact occurring in the presence of Mother's voice and smiling face conditions the baby to words as reinforcers.

Eventually when Mother smiles and says, "Good baby," the infant experiences a glow of satisfaction. This natural process of pairing food with physical contact along with smiles, tone of voice, gestures, and words results in satisfaction being produced by any of these occurring independently.

Talking to Baby paired with hugs, tickles, and bouncing or rocking becomes generalized, so that Baby responds to Father and other family members. Similarly, Baby learns to respond to others as he experiences satisfying interaction with an expanded community of individuals. In this way the foundation for all social satisfaction is established, and Baby learns to respond to a wide range of words and other expressions of social approval. He feels satisfaction when he receives approval and dissatisfaction in the presence of disapproval.

A baby is God's opinion that the world should go on.

— C. SANDBURG

As physical co-ordination develops, Baby holds a rattle or teething ring and derives satisfaction from manipulation of this object. He reaches for and holds a doll or stuffed toy and is pleased with this accomplishment. Through activities such as these, he obtains pleasure from toys and other objects and develops feelings of security in the presence of familiar things. He may become so attached to a blanket or stuffed toy that he takes it with him wherever he goes. Originally Baby derives satisfaction through manipulation of objects, and later a sense of possession develops so that a collection of objects may produce satisfaction.

What a man has, so much he is sure of.

— M. DE CERVANTES

Learning to walk provides satisfaction, and this pleasure is augmented by social approval. The child is reinforced by his successful mastery of his environment. Competent interactions with the physical world are both reinforcing and motivating. Operating a mechanical device, riding a tricycle or other conveyance, and exploring his environment provide satisfying and reinforcing experiences that increase his motivation to be competent.

> The great end of life is not knowledge but action.
>
> —T. Huxley

The young child becomes aware of the utility of money through observation and direct experience. When he exchanges a coin for the purchase of candy or ice cream he learns the power of a token. He exchanges a token, which

Operating a mechanical device provides satisfying and reinforcing experience.

originally has no value to him, for something which gives him satisfaction. After experience in exchanging money for goods such as food, toys, or service, such as rides or movies, receiving money will by itself provide satisfaction.

Any token system operates on the same principle, so that collecting poker chips, saving stamps, bonus coupons, coins, or anything else that can be exchanged will produce satisfaction.

> Ready money is Aladdin's lamp.
> —LORD BYRON

As the growing child interacts with his environment he receives feedback which influences his future behavior. When behavior produces feedback that is pleasant or satisfying, that behavior is strengthened in the future. When the behavior produces feedback that is unpleasant, painful, or unsatisfying, that behavior is weakened in the future. Behavior that produces no feedback tends to gradually disappear.

Satisfaction may come from any of the reinforcements: food, social approval, words of praise, material acquisitions, competence in environmental interaction, money or other tokens.

At school the feedback may consist of teacher praise, classmates' approval, check marks, gold stars, or marks and grades.

Status is another form of knowledge of results. The child wins a race, loses a contest, ranks in the top, middle, or bottom group in class. Status is symbolized by badges, medals, uniforms, winner ribbons, and report cards.

> "I'm just as big for me," said he,
> "As you are big for you!"
> —J. BANGS

Some children spontaneously begin to check their own work and evaluate how they are doing. In this case the

At school the feedback may consist of teacher praise.

child tells himself whether his behavior is acceptable. If he decides that he has done well, this produces the same internal satisfaction as the other reinforcers. It is the child's ability to reinforce himself through self-evaluation that maintains his behavior during those periods when Teacher's attention or other external reinforcement is not being continuously provided.

Self-evaluation, the highest level of reinforcement, is also called intrinsic reinforcement or self-motivation. Common statements used to describe the behavior of a person who is reinforced by self-evaluation are: "She works well on her own." "He takes responsibility for his job." "He lives up to his standards."

At the highest level of development of self-evaluation, the individual conceptualizes an ideal self based upon his social or philosophical formulations, and then evaluates his own behavior in relation to this ideal-self concept. This abstract level of reinforcement maintains behavior toward high ideals and in some cases produces internal satisfactions that outweigh externally imposed punishment.

> Know then this truth, enough for man to know,
> Virtue alone is happiness below.
>
> —A. POPE

The developmental acquisition of satisfaction or reinforcement starts with food and progresses through physical contact, words, social approval, material possessions, competent interactions with the environment, money and other token systems, knowledge of results, and self-evaluation. Each of these contains the earlier reinforcers, so that the developmental stages represent expanding repertoires of responsiveness to reinforcers.

The stages overlap and are not acquired in units. They are part of the total interdependent development of the individual personality. Each stage described herein is important to the development of the fully functioning human and all have application to systems of compensation.

The description so far is of the ideal development of a fully actualized individual who can set goals for himself, maintain progress toward those goals, evaluate his own performance, and make corrections to keep his life on that course. The person whose experiences have provided him with the opportunity to become this kind of complete human being is indeed fortunate. Parents vary greatly in their ability to provide an environment for this kind of development, and public education has failed to teach self-evaluation in a consistently effective way.

> Let no man presume to give advice to others
> that he has not first given counsel to himself.
>
> —SENECA

With many years' experience using a variety of reinforcement systems with children and university students and study of compensation systems in industry, I have developed the following Peter Prescriptions.

A pat on the back is only a few vertebrae removed from a kick in the pants, but is miles
ahead in results.

—V. WILCOX

PETER PRESCRIPTION 51
The Peter Pedagogy: *Reinforce the
child's every incidence of Humanite behavior*

Because a child's behavior is reinforced by appropriately
administered adult attention, teachers and parents can
strengthen creativity, confidence, and competence in children. Adult approval communicated to a child whenever
he behaves well academically and socially will increase
his Humanite development.

> There is nothing so much worth as a mind well
> instructed.
>
> —ECCLESIASTICUS

PETER PRESCRIPTION 52
The Peter Pair: *Present an effective reinforcer
along with the reinforcer you wish to develop*

Individuals not fortunate enough to have had the benefits
of Peter Pedagogue child-raising methods can be helped
through remedial action. With your understanding of the
developmental hierarchy of reinforcements you will be
able to establish effective reinforcement procedures for individuals who are unresponsive because of developmental
deprivations.

> Any critic can establish a wonderful batting
> average by just rejecting every new idea.
>
> —J. D. WILLIAMS

As a university professor working with doctoral students who were supposed to be capable of conducting independent study and research, I rarely found one who could evaluate his own work. Even with graduate students who had many years of training in a system that taught them simply to follow instructions and leave the evaluation to Teacher, I was able to achieve considerable success in fostering self-evaluation through re-education. I began by having the student define the objectives for his project, establish his criteria for successful completion, identify the checkpoints, and evaluate the project at each checkpoint. I then reinforced the student for his evaluation of his own performance. In other words, instead of providing reinforcement for doing the project the way I thought was best, I reinforced him for *his evaluation* of *his project* in terms of *his own criteria*. He received as much praise and academic credit for a favorable as for an unfavorable evaluation as long as the evaluation was consistent with his stated objective. This process helped the student toward independent self-evaluation.

> The common idea that success spoils people by making them vain, egotistic, and self-complacent is erroneous; on the contrary, it makes them, for the most part, humble, tolerant, and kind. Failure makes people cruel and bitter.
> —S. MAUGHAM

In the natural development of satisfactions from food and cuddling to knowledge of results and self-evaluation, pairing plays an important part. When Mother pairs feeding her baby with talking to it, her voice and words become stronger satisfiers. Later, in school, when Teacher pairs an effective reinforcer such as praise with the presentation of a check mark, the check mark increases in reinforcing value. Subsequently the check mark will be a stronger reinforcer of correct answers.

This pairing process applies throughout life. A flower presented to a loved one along with words of appreciation will take on increased satisfying value, so that the presentation of a flower in the future will produce a satisfying emotional response.

> What we most love and revere generally is determined by early associations.
> —O. W. HOLMES, JR.

Lowell Scorer took up golf primarily to be with some of his pals who enjoyed the game. He made rapid progress and soon gained the admiration of his friends for his excellent scores. Two events were paired—the admiration of his friends, and the improved score. Later, when he practiced golf alone, the satisfactory score he achieved gave him some of the same feelings he had experienced when he received the approval of his friends. Low Scorer was hooked on the game and was highly motivated to continue to improve.

> Applause is the only appreciated interruption.
> —A. GLASGOW

The Central Division of Grinn and Barret, Inc., had regressed until it had become a dehumanized component of a large corporation. Ben Ifitz was appointed divisional manager and soon discovered that his department heads and supervisors were ritualistically going through the motions of fulfilling the requirements of their jobs. He set about revitalizing the division.

He met individually with department heads and expressed his interest in their problems and aspirations. Sufficient time was spent with each to explore reasonable goals and criteria for assessing success. Each man was encouraged to develop a sequence of objectives and a system for rating progress toward them. In subsequent meetings Ifitz praised each man for his evaluation. The self-rating was paired with praise and in some cases extra privileges. This increased the satisfaction achieved through self-evaluation, which in turn increased motivation toward improved performance. Ben Ifitz then encouraged the department heads to develop similar types of self-rating through the participation of the supervisors and their staffs. Through this process he was able to increase motivation and feelings of involvement of the division personnel.

> Appreciation is a wonderful thing: it makes
> what is excellent in others belong to us as well.
> —F. VOLTAIRE

The motivation of employees involves a number of things, some within control of the manager and some outside of his control.

Constitutional factors, childhood experiences, and off-the-job activities of the employee influence motivation and are beyond the control of the manager.

The manager does have control over the most important influence on employee motivation: the granting and withholding of rewards.

> What one single ability do we all have? the
> ability to change.
> —L. ANDREWS

PETER PRESCRIPTION 53
The Peter Pay: *Make pay obtainable as a result of good job performance*

Research provides clear guides as to the kind of perception that must exist if pay is to be an effective motivator. Pay must be perceived as both important and obtainable. No matter how important pay is, it will not be a motivator unless it is perceived as relating to performance. In an organization where superior-subordinate relationships are characterized by mistrust, the subordinates will not perceive that rewards are contingent upon competence. If it is believed that being a yes-man, playing office politics, or being a relative or friend of the superior pays off, it matters not what the facts are. People are motivated by what they believe.

> Under certain conditions, men respond as powerfully to fictions as they do to realities, and in many cases, they help to create the very fictions to which they respond.
> —W. Lippmann

The value of money in motivating competence depends upon the needs it satisfies. Needs can be arranged in a hierarchy. At the bottom are basic survival needs, including physical well-being and security. In the middle are social needs—communication, love, recognition, esteem, and meaningful associations. At the top is self-actualization, including creativity, autonomy, and the self-realization of fully developing one's competence.

It is essential to understand this hierarchy, because as lower-level needs are satisfied, they become less important and higher-order needs become more important. The key question about the importance of pay concerns what needs it satisfies. Pay can buy food and satisfy certain security and physical needs. These are satisfied rather easily by most citizens. Once satisfied these needs become less important, so if pay satisfies only these it will not be an effective compensation for competence.

> Pay is a status symbol that can satisfy esteem and recognition needs and because of this be an important reward.
> —E. Lawler III

PETER PRESCRIPTION 54
The Peter Promotion: *Use promotion as a reward only when the promotee has shown capability for the new position*

It has been amply demonstrated that promotion as compensation for work well done does not ultimately produce competence, although it may provide some temporary benefits on the way up. Similarly, pay increases may work for a while, but it is evident that we have highly paid incompetent mechanics, teachers, tradesmen, physicians, engineers, administrators, and politicians. Money alone cannot produce competence.

In organizations employing a variety of professionals it is desirable to establish multiple promotion ladders. This provides for promotion within a professional category, so that a researcher or technical expert can be rewarded without moving him into management. Traditionally, promotion lacks the flexibility required of an effective reward system.

> We're overpaying him but he's worth it.
> —S. GOLDWYN

E. Z. Goze, a highly successful salesman with years of experience at Attit, Early and Layte Enterprises, was promoted to sales manager. Marginally competent in this position, he kept the sales division operating, but his organizing ability left much to be desired. Within six months of E. Z. Goze's promotion it was discovered that Red E. Aim, a highly competent and experienced salesman who had been with Attit, Early and Layte Enterprises Incorporated for two years, possessed outstanding organizational ability and leadership qualities. Red E. Aim's competence can be rewarded by his being promoted to manager in eleven years, when E. Z. retires.

They defend their errors as if they were defending their inheritance.

—E. Burke

In an efficient motivation system the rewards must appear to be within reach, must be perceived as contingent upon competent performance, and must be presented within reasonable time. In most situations it is only a coincidence when promotion meets these criteria.

The universe is full of magical things patiently waiting for our wits to grow sharper.

—E. Phillpotts

PETER PRESCRIPTION 55

The Peter Place: *Reinforce the competent employee by systematically increasing the status of the place in which he works*

Society has defined rank or status in many ways. Some tribal customs have included seating the chief on a larger rock. In other societies the chief's house or hut has had a distinctive design. A citizen's rank has been determined by the decoration and insignia on his house, the height of his bed, and the physical distance between his hut and that of the chief's.

The modern business establishment is organized in the same manner. The chief executive's office is placed in the most prestigious area of the building, usually the top floor. It is large, thickly carpeted, and elegantly furnished with a huge desk and spacious chairs. Moving down the hierarchy, the offices are smaller, the furniture cheaper, and the carpets thinner.

In business, industry, civil service, and education there are many opportunities to reinforce competence by improving the quality, comfort, or status of the worker's environment. The competent mechanic can be rewarded by allowing him to choose his bench or work station. In large establishments offices are a source of status, and items such as the following are used to indicate rank:

> name painted on glass panel of office door
> name on door printed in gold leaf
> name engraved in brass plate on door
> partial glass partition
> partitions that reach the ceiling
> size of office
> size of window
> having a window
> draperies for window
> floor covering
> office equipment

This incomplete list will give some idea of the possibilities for reinforcing competence through increasing the status value of the employee's work station. The traditional bigger office, with outer office and secretary, may be part of the motivation of the upwardly mobile, ambitious individual, but application of the Peter Place provides many more gradations and possibilities for reward without removing the competent employee from his place.

> We shape our buildings; thereafter they shape us.
>
>   —W. Churchill

A review of the performance of department manager Ernest A. Peale showed that he had competently fulfilled his objectives. As Peale stepped into his office, his foot sank into carpeting that had just been installed. No words needed to be spoken. He knew that his competence was appreciated. He felt secure. His confidence increased with every footstep. A few months later his continued competent performance was rewarded when he drove his car into a reserved parking space with his name on it. Following each evaluation period showing the effectiveness of his management, Peale was reinforced by the Peter Place. After one particularly effective management decision he received the ultimate—a key to the executive washroom.

Nothing is new except arrangement.
—W. DURANT

The available array of telephones and telephone appliances, office furniture, desk sets, desk signs, inscribed pens, ash trays, chairs, art objects, framed awards, and certificates of merit makes it possible to maintain this schedule of reinforcement for many years without undue repetition. By that time some of the equipment and furnishings will be out of date and you can start over again.

The Peter Place provides a means of reinforcement that rewards an employee at his level of competence. The application of this Peter Prescription* requires sensitivity and an innovative approach. Traditionally, it is considered efficient to standardize all offices at each rank. Noncontingent status of work stations achieves a small saving in maintenance that is more than offset by loss of competence.

Contentment, rosy, dimpled maid,
Thou brightest daughter of the sky.
—L. MANNERS

* A reverse application of the Peter Place has been employed as a dehiring procedure. The superior decides that he has promoted a subordinate beyond his level of competence. Firing the subordinate would cast suspicion on the superior's earlier judgment. His immediate objective is to get the subordinate to resign. Monday morning the subordinate arrives at work, and as he steps into his office his foot receives a message that is transmitted to his total nervous system. The underfelt has been removed from beneath the carpet. Tuesday morning he discovers that his name has been taken from the door. By Friday, when he arrives to find that his desk has been removed, he is already looking for another job.

PETER PRESCRIPTION 56
The Peter Performance: *Encourage employees to believe that rewards are based upon performance*

For rewards to be motivators of competence, an essential condition is that the rewards be seen by employees as tied to performance. The manager has limited control over whether rewards will be important to the individuals within an organization, but rewards for competence consistent with stated compensation policy will create motivation based upon compensation tied to performance.

Pleasure is due only when all duty's done.
—R. POLLOK

Jake Bilgewater, president of Belchfire Rocket Boat Company, told me that he and his top management had developed the fairest and most attractive system of bo-

Pleasure is due only when all duty's done.

nuses that his company could afford. He was disappointed in its ineffectiveness and had heard that the men regarded it as a joke.

My survey of Belchfire personnel indicated that the men perceived the bonus system as just another way for old Bilgewater to give raises to his relatives and friends who held most of the key positions in the firm.

> If you're not able to communicate successfully between yourself and yourself, how are you supposed to make it with the strangers outside?
> —J. FEIFFER

PETER PRESCRIPTION 57
The Peter Proposition: *Provide discriminable differences between the rewards given for good and poor performance*

If rewards are to be tied to performance, they should be large enough to be recognized. This applies to pay as well as to all other reward systems.

It is ineffective to give incompetent employees a 5 percent annual raise and competent employees a 10 percent raise. No matter what is said in behalf of such a financial pat on the head, it has not been found effective as a motivator and as a reinforcer of competence.

> He who praises everybody praises nobody.
> —S. JOHNSON

O. C. Bigman, president of Wrapture, Inc., the wrapping and packaging division of Doo and Daire Enterprises, was aware that the best employees on a given job produced at least twice as much as the worst employee doing the same job. He decided to apply the Peter Proposition by dividing each employee's pay into three parts. The first part of the pay was based on the job the employee was doing, so that everyone holding a position with the same job classification received the same amount for this part of his pay. The second part was based upon seniority and the cost of living. Every employee received this part of the pay package adjusted automatically each year. The third part was not automatic—it was adjusted so that each employee's pay was based upon his individual performance during the preceding period.

The most incompetent performer at Wrapture, Inc., received nothing for this part of his pay, while the most competent received as much for this part of his pay as the other two parts combined. O. C. Bigman made it clear that this was not a raise and would vary, based on the employee's performance during the preceding period. Salary increases came only with changes in job classification, cost of living, and seniority.

The merit portion of pay varied, so that if performance decreased pay also decreased. As the employees saw that those doing good work were rewarded, they accepted the fact that a real merit reward system existed at Wrapture, Inc.

> Strengthen me by sympathizing with my strengths not my weakness.
>
> —B. Alcott

PETER PRESCRIPTION 58
The Peter Profit: *Make the total operation a co-operative enterprise by sharing the profits with the employees*

> Let every man be respected as an individual and no man idolized.
>
> —A. Einstein

PETER PRESCRIPTION 59
The Peter Protection: *Make fringe benefits provide real security and meaningful prestige*

Competence can be reinforced by providing security and prestige through additional fringe benefits. Extra fringe benefits as compensation for competent performance can be effective motivators and reinforcers at all levels of the hierarchy. In most business establishments only executives are provided with company limousines, unlimited expense accounts, husband-wife business trips abroad, stock options, and club memberships. This is justified in terms of the need to help executives build proprietary interest in their companies. What is more, additional noncash compensation for the executives receiving high salaries takes advantage of loopholes in the income-tax regulations.

When the fringe benefits actually provide security or prestige and are contingent upon competence, they can be effective. Unfortunately they frequently fail to meet these requirements.

He is well paid that is well satisfied.
—W. SHAKESPEARE

B. Eager, an up-and-coming young executive, was promoted to the status of regional vice-president of Watch and Wayte Products, Limited. This new position provided his first entry into the company's management-incentive program, including an option on ten thousand shares of stock. B. Eager was eager to show his gratitude and faith in Watch and Wayte, so he purchased the ten thousand shares with his savings and a bank loan. The stock-market slump that reduced the value of the stock by 50 percent was not related to his competence or his loyalty to Watch and Wayte Products.

> Next to knowing when to seize an opportunity,
> the most important thing in life is to know
> when to forgo an advantage.
> —B. DISRAELI

Ivan Austin accepted a promotion which required that he move from Santa Cruz, California, to the head office in New York. He received an increase in salary that was wiped out by the increased cost of living. He also received a company limousine, which he seldom used. It took so long to thread his way through nerve-racking crosstown traffic each day that after the first week he gave up and took the commuter train, thereby saving time and what remained of his nervous system.

> He worked like hell in the country so he could
> live in the city, where he worked like hell so
> he could live in the country.
> —D. MARQUIS

PETER PRESCRIPTION 60
The Peter Pantry: *Allow each employee to select the compensation benefits he or she would like to achieve*

The idea of offering employees a choice of the form their compensation will take has gained wide acceptance among compensation experts, management consultants, behavioral scientists, employees, and union leaders.

By providing a pantry with a wide selection of food you can satisfy nearly anyone's appetite. Similarly, it is possible to stock your compensation shelves with rewards which will meet the pay, prestige, security, or self-fulfilment needs of your employees.

Offering a young employee struggling to buy a home and raise a family a choice of stock-option plans, retirement benefits, and country-club memberships may be a poor incentive plan. None of these noncash compensations meet any of his immediate needs. Later, during mid-career, these compensations may be very attractive to him. Compensation options should include cash bonuses, increased holidays, opportunities to select projects or do creative work, and a wide selection of fringe benefits.

The Peter Pantry, otherwise known as the "cafeteria method of compensation" or the "supermarket concept," has the advantage of individualizing compensation through the employee's own choice. At various times throughout his career the employee can select the compensation benefits that meet his needs and for which he is willing to put forth his most competent effort.

> Now is the time for all good men to come to the aid of themselves.
> —F. NELSON

PETER PRESCRIPTION 61
The Peter Purpose: *Motivate and reinforce employees by accurately communicating what they are to achieve and provide feedback that communicates how well they are achieving that objective*

Clearly defined objectives communicate to the employee what he is supposed to achieve, and provide a basis for an objective evaluation of his performance.

When Ryte Onn, an experienced wheel tapper for the Toonerville Central Railway, was asked why he went around tapping wheels, he replied, "I don't know."

> Letting down buckets into empty wells, and growing old with drawing nothing up.
> —W. COWPER

PETER PRESCRIPTION 62
The Peter Participation: *Reward group performance*

For many individuals the strongest motivators are the challenge of the job and the opportunities to achieve something and to associate with people they admire.

Sometimes it is not practical to measure individual performance. Under these conditions it makes sense to use group performance as a basis for rewarding employees. Group-reward plans motivate co-operative behavior.

> No member of a crew is praised for the rugged individuality of his rowing.
>
> —R. W. EMERSON

The installation of an assembly line at Trojan Traction Tractors had originally improved production, but in recent years more and more tractors were being completed with parts missing. It appeared that workers were becoming bored with repeating the same operation over and over. The first solution the company tried was to increase the number of inspectors. The inspectors soon became bored with the repetitive nature of their jobs, and defective tractors began receiving the inspectors' stamp of approval.

I. C. Lyte, a competent industrial engineer, redesigned the assembly procedure and organized the men into platoons, each of which was responsible for the assembly of a major component. One group assembled the transmission, another installed the electrical systems, and so forth. Each platoon received bonuses for the absence of defects for their component reported during the warranty period.

Co-operative behavior flourished. Defects practically disappeared. Boredom was eliminated. Creative involvement of the employees in improving both procedures and product was evident.

> Men build too many walls and not enough bridges.   —D. PIRE

PETER PRESCRIPTION 63
The Peter Power: *Compensate competent performance by providing opportunities for individual initiative*

Many competent people feel great frustration because of rules and bureaucratic restrictions. Frustration can frequently be replaced with satisfaction when the competent employee is granted the authority to utilize his power to do his job or manage his department in his own way. In this manner attention is focused on realistic objectives rather than upon ritualistic procedures. Improved effectiveness follows when administrators show respect for competent people and translate that respect into patterns of freedom to use individual initiative. This satisfies the need for self-fulfillment and for feeling esteemed and valued.

> Individuality is everywhere to be spared and respected as the root of everything good.
> —J. RICHTER

PETER PRESCRIPTION 64
The Peter Praise: *Communicate approval for specific acts of competence*

Administration is defined as a process of organizing, deputizing, supervising, decision making, programming, coordinating, appraising, and controlling. Most definitions omit the most important ingredient, a way of working with people to fulfill objectives. This way of working requires sympathetic understanding, empathy, good will, friendliness, and compassion.

We all value praise or approval according to the source from which it comes. When you are praised by someone you distrust you may feel that he is attempting to put something over.

> We sometimes imagine we hate flattery, but we
> only hate the way we are flattered.
>
> —F. LA ROCHEFOUCAULD

M. T. Hart was an administrator who cherished his authority and status. He concentrated his attention on planning, organizing, commanding, and controlling. He felt that subordinates existed to carry out the directions and schedules he handed down. When a colleague discussed the importance of human relations in administration, M. T. Hart remarked, "Nice guys finish last."

M. T. attended a seminar on behavior modification and was impressed with the research results that were reported. He left the seminar elated because he had learned a new technique for bending his subordinates to his will. For the next two weeks he watched for any employee's performance that would enhance M. T.'s status and lavished praise on the startled subordinate. In almost every case the subordinate became immediately suspicious of M. T.'s intentions and feared the resentment of coworkers.

> Even in politics, an evil action has evil conse-
> quences. That, I believe, is the law of Nature
> as precise as any law of physics or chemistry.
>
> —J. NEHRU

Frank N. Able was an administrator who kept a balance between consideration for individuals and emphasis on getting the job done. In his day-to-day activities he showed genuine concern for the comfort and welfare of his subordinates. He willingly participated with them in eliminating problems. His praise and approval were effective reinforcers of competent performance.

> It gives pleasure to be praised by one whom all
> men praise.
>
> —T. HOWE

PETER PRESCRIPTION 65
The Peter Prestige: *Communicate with competent subordinates in all ranks*

Association with prestigious persons is sought by nearly everyone. Crowds gather to see, touch, or shake hands with a successful entertainer, author, or politician. Within an organization, association and communication with the top executive are highly rewarding.

Traditional hierarchies are organized so that communication flows downward through levels of authority. The most competent as well as the most incompetent at any level communicates only vertically with the rank above.

By turning the traditional administration chart on its side there would be more provision for promotion within

Association with prestigious persons is sought by nearly everyone.

ranks and more rewards for individuals within their levels of competence. Within this rotated hierarchy those who rise to the top of each rank, through competence within that rank, would be in closer communication with the top of all ranks. This would be a powerful incentive for the most competent to stay in his rank and maintain competence. If he were promoted to the next rank he would lose status and might never be able to achieve a position in the top group of his new rank.

In the rotated hierarchy the top executives would have direct access to the most competent individuals in each rank. This communication would be an added prestige reinforcer for each rank and also provide the policy-making executives with the most direct, competent, and realistic advice from all ranks.

The whole is simpler than the sum of its parts.
                                                        —W. GIBBS

PETER PRESCRIPTION 66

The Peter Proximity: *Shape behavior by reinforcing successive approximations toward a desired objective*

All the compensation methods presented so far utilize shared objectives. It is perfectly ethical for a manager to reward an individual for achievement agreed upon and desired by that individual. Because the Peter Proximity does not always involve shared objectives, you must answer the question about your right to change another person's behavior. I have used the Peter Proximity for improving the behavior of retarded, psychotic, neurologically impaired, and other severely handicapped individuals referred to me for remedial instruction. I have always felt that I was justified in helping these individuals even though they were incapable of establishing objectives for themselves.

> In matters of conscience, the law of the majority has no place.
>
> —M. Gandhi

Because behavior is shaped by its consequences it can be systematically improved. Behavior followed immediately by reinforcement tends to be the behavior that occurs in the future. Because most human behavior is not repeated in exactly the same way each time, it is possible to shape behavior toward a desired objective. This is achieved by taking advantage of the variance in human behavior and reinforcing only the desired responses.

> There is nothing in the world constant, but inconstancy.
>
> —J. Swift

D. V. Jones, president of Excelsior City's famous Kon Tiki Boat Works, appointed his son-in-law, Noah Count, to the parts department. D. V. Jones expected Gene Yuss, parts supervisor, to teach Noah Count how to handle requisitions and routine procedures of the department. It was not long before Gene Yuss realized what a serious challenge D. V. Jones had given him.

After repeated careful explanations and demonstrations Noah still failed to mark the tallies in the stock bins, wrote entries on stock lists in the wrong columns, and made unintelligible notations. After consideration of the problem Gene Yuss decided to shape Noah's behavior toward acceptable performance levels. He defined exactly what Noah would have to do to be competent. He then took every opportunity to compliment Noah for every move in the direction of the competence objective. When Noah made a notation that was legible, Gene complimented him, pointing out that neatness and clarity made

this particular notation readable. Gene systematically reinforced Noah's best performance in each task until,
through approximations, satisfactory performance was
achieved. Gene Yuss realized that if he had waited for
Noah Count to perform a complete task competently, he
might have waited indefinitely.

> He hath riches sufficient, who hath enough
> to be charitable.
>
> —SIR T. BROWNE

We have seen that Peter Prescriptions can be used to
promote quality performance. Although management techniques have traditionally been used mainly by business,
they have an important contribution to make to politics,
education, civil rights, or any other endeavor where human behavior must be influenced to achieve worthwhile
objectives.

> Don't forget until too late that the business of
> life is not business, but living.
>
> —B. C. FORBES

Au Revoir
or
The Peter Plan

Ideas won't keep: something must be done
about them.

—A. N. WHITEHEAD

Au Revoir
or
The Peter Plan

Ah! when shall all men's good
Be each man's rule, and universal peace
Lie like a shaft of light across the land?
—A. TENNYSON

APPREHENSION about the future increasingly corrodes modern life. We have become locked into institutional habits, permitting technological and organizational techniques to become the determinants of social change. Hierarchies have become self-perpetuating, so that their power increases as responsibility and individual identity decreases. Hierarchal Regression has eroded qualitative standards. The gross national product is still the official indicator of national achievement. It lumps together the total dollars of cigarette commercials and cancer treatment, automobile sales and mortuary fees, napalm and healing drugs.

The cost of living is going up and the chance of living is going down.
—F. (FLIP) WILSON

Mindless escalation of the use of power has encouraged modern man to believe that he is above nature and that he can dictate to the natural world without respect for the ecological consequences. The rape and exploitation of seemingly boundless land and natural beauty continues as the ugly consequences become more and more apparent.

Although other issues have diverted our attention, the possibility of a cataclysmic war remains so long as national defense is based upon atomic threat and mutual-deterrence systems. Today, when a war might wipe out the entire human race, we need effective international law and peace-keeping procedures to make war impossible.

> Taking an active part in the solutions of the problems of peace is a moral duty which no conscientious man can shirk.
>
> —A. EINSTEIN

A large segment of youth realizes that it is culturally unassimilated in a civilization of endless congestion and incredibly ineffectual approaches to living. Some have tried to escape to agrarian communes in an effort to forge a oneness with the land, while others are caught up in the rhetoric of revolution. Ironically, while youth is attacked by the establishment, there is growing support elsewhere for youth's positions on social justice, environmental quality, survival, and peace.

> If we wish to make a new world, we have the materials ready—the first one too was made out of chaos.
>
> —R. QUILLEN

Application of the Peter Prescriptions is the first step in reversing escalatory entrapment. Each individual who applies Peter Prescriptions contributes to his own fulfillment as a Humanite and to the survival of the human race.

He who reforms himself has done more towards reforming the public than a crowd of noisy, impotent patriots.

—J. LAVATER

Technological progress is not inherently evil, but when it develops without corresponding social, educational, and humanistic advances, the system becomes glutted. *The Peter Prescription* presents a means by which each of us can begin the reconstructive planning of society. Man cannot live by incompetence alone.

The supreme question before mankind—to which I shall not live to know the answer—is how men will be able to make themselves willing and able to save themselves.

—W. LIPPMANN

Man cannot live by incompetence alone.

A NOTE ON THE ILLUSTRATIONS

The author and the publisher of *The Peter Prescription* wish to thank A. V. Caudery, Chairman of *Punch*, for permission to use the illustrations with which this book is decorated. For anyone who might be interested, we list as follows the names of the artists and the original dates of publication:

Page
10 A. C. Courbould (May 3, 1884)
14 G. du Maurier (April 2, 1887)
23 W. Ralston (February 22, 1879)
26 G. du Maurier (November 28, 1885)
29 G. du Maurier (August 8, 1874)
37 G. du Maurier (October 20, 1885)
39 G. du Maurier (November 2, 1889)
43 G. du Maurier (February 4, 1888)
53 G. du Maurier (July 12, 1879)
59 G. du Maurier (September 9, 1876)
63 C. du Maurier (January 11, 1879)
75 G. du Maurier (September 3, 1881)
79 G. du Maurier (September 21, 1889)
88 Charles Keene (February 18, 1882)
104 Charles Keene (March 15, 1873)
113 G. du Maurier (October 30, 1880)
122 Charles Keene (October 1, 1881)
126 G. du Maurier (June 16, 1877)
140 G. du Maurier (August 6, 1881)
149 E. T. Reed (December 6, 1890)
153 A. C. Courbould (February 28, 1885)
158 A. C. Courbould (July 11, 1885)
169 G. du Maurier (February 5, 1881)
172 Charles Keene (October 30, 1880)
175 G. du Maurier (May 29, 1880)